Magical Marketing

Magical Marketing

◆

19 Marketing Secrets to Turbo-charge Your Business within the Next 7 Days.

Andrew Lock

iUniverse, Inc.
New York Lincoln Shanghai

Magical Marketing
19 Marketing Secrets to Turbo-charge Your Business within the Next 7 Days.

iUniverse, Inc.

For information address:
iUniverse, Inc.
2021 Pine Lake Road, Suite 100
Lincoln, NE 68512
www.iuniverse.com

The companies and businesses that are referred to in this book are cited as examples of what can be achieved with effective marketing campaigns. Any cited or perceived negative connotation is no reflection on the current success of the businesses referred to, and no malice is intended. The author does not recommend one business over another in any particular area, and any comparisons are made purely for the purposes of learning marketing lessons. This book contains the opinions of the author.

Many trademarks, brand names and corporate identities have been referred to throughout the text. The author acknowledges that these remain the property of the owners.

ISBN: 0-595-30942-9

Printed in the United States of America

Contents

The majority of small businesses fail within their first three years.

Why?

Often, it comes down to an inability *to market their products or services effectively. Magical Marketing* provides the solution to this problem.

Whether you are starting from scratch or have an existing business, *Magical Marketing* will refocus your attention on the critical need for effective marketing. More than that, it will direct you step-by-step through each process necessary to ensure that orders start to flood in.

Armed with the 19 proven marketing strategies contained within, small business owners can dramatically increase their sales within just seven days.

Introduction

If you have a great product or service, you are guaranteed to make a lot of money, right? Wrong! The reality is that many superb products and services continually fall by the wayside simply because not enough people know they exist, and even if they do know they exist, they are not aware of *why* they should buy them. Fortunately, there is a solution…

Enter "marketing," a well known but frequently misunderstood word from the world of business. It encompasses promotion, advertising, publicizing, and selling. Marketing lets potential buyers know that a product or service exists that can benefit them, and it provides powerful reasons why they should spend their money on it.

When carried out properly as part of a well thought out campaign, marketing is highly persuasive—it encourages potential customers to buy something that they probably had not planned to buy. Think about that last statement carefully. The ability to persuade someone to buy something that they had probably not planned to buy is arguably more valuable than 99% of other business skills. Remember, customers are the lifeblood of any business. Without them your business is as good as dead.

It follows that if marketing is ignored, sales will be dramatically reduced compared to what they could and should be. Whereas it is possible to sell a poor product with good marketing, it is far more difficult if not impossible to sell a great product without it. That's how important marketing is.

In simple terms, trying to run a business without marketing is like trying to drive a car that has no fuel. The car may be equipped in every other way, but without the fuel it will stay motionless forever. Marketing is the fuel of business. It provides the power, the driving force that will enable your company to move forward.

Whilst most business owners realise the need for marketing, that acknowledgment rarely gets translated into an *effective* marketing strategy. More often that not, many small companies think that marketing means placing an occasional advert, sending out some sales letters, and spending lots of money on an initial product launch. Much more is needed however, in order to succeed and profit in today's competitive business climate.

1

Let's come back to the popular belief that the product or service in itself is the most important thing, and that sales will follow automatically. This is a misguided view that is held by many small businesses owners. This over confident view is dangerous. Some business owners genuinely believe that because they have a superior product or service, they will *automatically* blow the competition out of the water. However, even if all the indications are that your product will "fly out the door," this will not be the case unless you have a well thought out and implemented marketing strategy.

The Sony Betamax Lesson

One of the most prominent examples of a marketing disaster was the ill-fated Sony Betamax consumer video format. Launched in 1976, the Betamax video recorders initially sold well. Advertising of the product was drastically cut back within a very short period however, and later in 1976, JVC launched the VHS format with a well-planned, continuous marketing campaign that literally swamped the market from every conceivable angle. Much of the marketing was very different from anything that had been tried previously, and the bold but structured approach really paid off.

At the time, industry experts generally agreed that the Sony format was technically superior compared to the VHS rival, yet we all know that the VHS format eventually won the day. Why? As noted, it was largely due to a more effective marketing campaign by JVC, the creators of VHS. They literally used every means at their disposal to promote the format, and crucially they appealed directly to the right target audience in a very powerful way. One example of the creative approach to selling the product was the way that VHS recorders were stocked in supermarkets for the first time, encouraging customers to buy on impulse, along with their regular weekly shopping. Previously, video recorders had only been sold via specialist Audio-Video stores. Of course, we are now used to the concept of supermarkets selling all sorts of non-food products (and services), but at the time the approach was truly innovative, and highly effective.

Sony ultimately relented in the format war, in fact they started producing VHS recorders too (they had little choice considering that VHS players commanded 95% of the market at the time). So although Sony eventually got back on the right track, their early marketing mistakes cost them dearly.

As a postscript to the Sony example, it is interesting to note that when recordable consumer DVD technology first entered onto the scene, another format war seemed inevitable, with two main competing formats, +R and -R. Both formats worked well, but the two were incompatible with each other. What did Sony do? They designed a recorder that could handle both formats! Now that's a sensible solution!

Sony is now considered to be a leading force in marketing consumer electronics, and the company is frequently noted for its innovative and dynamic approach. Perhaps the Betamax lesson proved to be a powerful motivating force not to let anything like that happen again?

How You can Benefit from this Book

So now that you are convinced about the importance of marketing, what exactly is the purpose of this book? Well, having long been fascinated with the broad subject of selling, it became apparent to me that large companies spend a fortune on developing marketing strategies that will sell more products, and overtake the competition. The aim in writing the book was to compile and provide a single resource of marketing ideas that are proven to work—concepts and plans that you can immediately apply, without having to spend a lot of money. Many of them won't cost you anything but a few hours of your time. Some are so obvious that you will have completely missed them. Others are "secret" strategies that are generally not known.

As you read, it will be tempting to dismiss certain ideas and concepts as not relevant to your business. This may especially be the case when it comes to suggestions that seem obvious to you. Before you disregard any suggestion however, ask yourself: Am I using this idea? Have I actually implemented it and tried it? If not, stop bemoaning the fact that you already know of the concept, and do something about using it!

Of course, large companies run their businesses very differently from a sole trader or a small concern. Don't worry about that, because the main *principles* from each example are extracted for you, and suggestions are made as to how you can adapt and apply these principles in your own business, which we assume to be relatively small.

You now have access to some of the most powerful marketing concepts and practical solutions that have ever been devised. The key is to implement as many as you can. Theory is fine, but it's what you do with it that counts. Reading about a marketing concept, and thinking about how good it is, will not bring in any more customers. What counts is putting it into practice, and you will be so glad you did! If you are serious about your business, you will take marketing seriously. Remember, the bottom line is your profit. That's what is at stake. Well thought out marketing, implemented effectively, _will_ have a magical effect on your profits.

Something else that ought to be mentioned is that there may appear to be a contradiction in the advice that is given. On the one hand it is recommended that you follow marketing strategies from well known companies, but you will also read that you should stand out as different from others. Actually, there is no contradiction. The ideas that have been singled out in this book are here *because* they are different from the norm, so you *will* benefit by adapting them to suit your own business. Yes, you *will* be following the approach of others in some cases, but *you will not be following the majority*, and that's the key difference.

How Should the Book be Read?

Some readers may wish to read the book from cover to cover in a methodical way, but it's worth noting that the format means that it's not necessary to do so. You are encouraged to read every page of course, because you simply don't know what will spark off an effective marketing idea. Sometimes, a concept that you may initially dismiss out of hand will jumble around in your mind for awhile, and suddenly you will have a flash of inspiration, becoming excited at the way an idea could be adapted for your business.

If your time is limited, one suggestion that you may want to implement is to read and carefully consider *just one* marketing strategy from the book each week. That way, as you go about your daily business you will have time to meditate on how the principle or method can be used to increase sales in your business.

Enjoy reading, and I look forward to hearing of your successes. If you would like to contact me directly, please feel free to do so. My email address is: andrewlock@socal.rr.com

1

Offer Something Free!

◆

How a four letter word can increase sales

Humans are funny creatures. Seeing the word "free" displayed in connection with an offer can suddenly transform rational, reserved individuals, into animated, excited, even obsessive ones.

The notion of getting something for nothing has a universal appeal, and it's often amusing to see the extraordinary lengths that some people go to in order to benefit from a "free" offer, whilst apparently ignoring the time and money that they spent in the process!

If you have ever experienced the grand opening of a new supermarket, you may have seen this for yourself. On such occasions, the store naturally wants to entice customers and ensure a flurry of activity for their opening day, so offering freebies, giveaways, prizes and so on, usually has the desired effect. People have been known to camp out the night before, travel from a neighbouring town, take a day off work and so on—because they have been influenced by a four letter word—FREE!

Of course, rarely is something offered completely free, without any strings attached. As the saying goes, "There is no such thing as a free lunch." Normally something, albeit small, is required in return, whether it is completing a survey, buying another product (as in buy one get one free), agreeing to receive a quotation, and so on. Having said that, let's re-emphasise that just seeing the word free causes many people to take notice—they often conveniently overlook any requirement in order to benefit from the "free" offer.

One company that has used the word "free" very effectively is AOL, the Internet service provider. Since the early to mid 1990's, AOL started sending out millions of CD's, either by mail or glued to the front cover of magazines. Each CD was a software installation disc, the aim being for the recipient to install AOL's proprietary brand of Internet access.

There were several clever elements to AOL's strategy. Firstly, for the most part they sent out the discs in DVD cases. This gave the package a high perceived value, and provided more room for a marketing message. Secondly, the offer was for a free trial, often for over a thousand hours of free Internet time. The combination of the two principles worked very effectively to the extent that some sources credit AOL with single-handedly popularising the Internet.

Companies such as BMG Music in the USA, and Britannia in the UK, have both used "free" offers as a central part of their marketing strategy. Both of these companies sell music CD's via mail order. They typically place adverts in magazines and on the Internet that offer a number of "free" CD's when a customer joins their music discount club. This has proved very effective.

Another way to make use of the word free in marketing is to offer a free trial. Oreck, the American based vacuum company have long realised the value in offering a free trial of their products. Although *they* know that they have an excellent range of vacuum cleaners, they exist in a highly competitive marketplace, so they had to find a way of separating themselves from the crowd.

The marketing message that Oreck puts out is very strong. They say something along the lines of, "We think Oreck products are the best. That's why we want you to try them in your own home, on your toughest cleaning problems, risk-free for 30 days. If you don't love the Oreck product you've purchased, you don't keep it. Simply send it back, no questions asked—you pay no return shipping costs." To an undecided customer, that offer is very attractive, because it removes any perceived element of risk.

So in marketing, the word "free" has tremendous power to influence consumers. It is perhaps the most useful marketing word at your disposal, as it *always* attracts attention.

Applying the principles to your business:

There are many ways you can use free offers to build a higher level of sales. Let's consider some of these…

If your product or service lends itself to doing so, give away free samples to your target audience. If you are selling a service, you could offer a free trial, if it is a product, it will probably be an actual sample of the product.

Costco the wholesale warehouse company are a good example of this. They regularly arrange, and offer, a free tasting of food and beverage products, as they know that there is nothing like actually trying a product to encourage people to buy it. Crucially though, Costco ensures that it is easy for customers to buy the product on impulse by making ample supplies available in store, near the tasting area. It is amazingly common to see companies handing out free samples of their product, without any information on how or where to buy more! So even if you tried it, and liked it, you might have to search hard in order to find it again.

It follows then that if you do decide to offer free samples, you must *make it easy for customers to buy in the future; in* fact it is imperative if you want to attract future sales. One excellent technique is to give a money-off coupon with each sample. As well as the discount however, the coupon has details of the company website, a brief sales blurb, and details of the main stockists. Although discount coupons are not as effective as free samples, they are still very effective, so the combination of the two offers at the same time is a great marketing strategy.

What if your product or service does not lend itself to giving a sample away, perhaps in the case of a high priced product for example? You can still offer free-bies or giveaways in the form of branded promotional items, such as pens, mugs, mouse-mats, key rings and so on—anything that the recipient is likely to use, and remember you for. If you are considering having such items made for you, don't rely on the manufacturer to advise you on what will be effective. In the majority of cases, they won't know what will be best for your business. My experience is that these types of businesses are only intent on "box shifting" a volume of prod-ucts, and they are rarely marketing experts.

What Sort of Promotional Items Should You Offer?

It is often tempting to go for the easy option of pens or mugs, or those kinds of items, because that is what everyone else does. Herein lies a powerful lesson. Don't follow the crowd, stand out as different, and you are far more likely to get noticed. Try and choose products that relate to your business in some way. If you are in the computer industry then a mouse-mat is very applicable. If you are in the catering industry then a mug is appropriate. You get the idea. Use your initia-tive, and remember that there are thousands of products available to you that can be branded with your companies' details. Be creative and dare to be different!

Make Sure Your Customers Know what You are Promoting!

For the moment, let's use the example of promotional mugs. It is common to see just the name of a company emblazoned on the side, and nothing else. Doing that is a recipe for a marketing disaster. Unless the recipient is a regular, loyal customer, six months down the line they won't have a clue what your company offers.

Even if the name of the company indicates the nature of the business, it is simply not enough to put this on its own. For example, I saw some promotional mugs that had "S.E.S." in large letters around the outside. Admittedly, in small print below, you could read the phrase "Southern Engraving Services." So at least that was a start. But what do they engrave? Tombstones? Signs? Silverware? Are they specialists in a particular field or industry, or do they offer a range of services? We'll never know, because there were no telephone numbers or website address included. In fact, there was no contact information at all, so even if you wanted something engraved, you would have a struggle to track the company down! This probably seems obvious reading this scenario, but look out for this marketing blunder over the next few months, and you'll find plenty of other examples, I assure you.

So it really is vital to include contact information on promotional items. Obviously, if you are considering ordering small promo items like pens, you will not be able to have all your details printed on them, so in that situation you should choose the most appropriate for your type of business. If you have a good web presence then I highly recommend that you feature your website, as it will act as a mini sales tool for you. Alternatively, simply put your telephone number.

On larger items (where you have more space for text), it is very helpful to have a marketing "strap line," which is a simple phrase that conveys what your company offers. An example would be, "Chase Couriers—Guaranteed next day delivery anywhere in the U.S." Another example might be: "First Choice Travel Agents—Specialists in low cost business travel." Can you see how much more effective your promotional material can be when you include a specific benefit?

Offer Free Shipping as an Occasional Offer to Valued Customers.

Free shipping is a great way of boosting sales from established customers. How can you go about this? You should be in regular contact with your customers as a matter of course. This is an area that we will expand upon later, but for now let's consider the basics. Communication with customers may be via fax, email, direct mail, even by telephone occasionally. Choose a medium that is most suited to your customer base. The communication should be personalised if possible, and always friendly.

Remember, customers are the lifeblood of your business. Yes, sometimes they are pain in the neck when they make unreasonable demands, and you may find it helpful to remember this quote: "Your customers are NOT always right, but they ARE always your customers."

Coming back to the main point, as part of your regular communication with customers, try offering them free shipping for a specified period, on orders over a certain value (you want to encourage the larger orders). If you have a good relationship with your customers, this will enhance that bond even further. They will feel as though they are receiving special treatment, and that's exactly what you want.

Some companies offer a "free shipping weekend," and that seems to work well, because at the weekends people tend to have more spare time, they are more relaxed, and ultimately more likely to spend their money. It doesn't have to be completely free shipping of course. If your shipping costs are very high, you might offer half price shipping, or make the offer a little different, such as "1 cent (or 1p) shipping this weekend." What counts is that your customers perceive they are valued, and that you are giving them special treatment. Even if the actual savings they are likely to receive are small (which is probably the case), the customer will still feel that they have received something for nothing, and psychologically that is a powerful proposition.

Several companies that I advised to implement this strategy, reported around a 1/3 increase in sales during the period that they tried it, and the slight decrease in profit from each transaction was more than compensated for by the substantial increase in sales.

How to use the Word "FREE" in Internet Based Businesses.

If your business is primarily online, there are still opportunities to use the word "free." Some websites have a request form, where visitors can enter their details, in order to obtain a free sample, newsletter, quotation, tour of a subscriber's part of the website, or simply free information.

If you go down this route, bear in mind that most people will find a long, complicated form very daunting, and they will not spend the time to complete it, unless they are very serious. In this sense, forms are sometimes a mixed blessing, and you need to find the right balance. Why? On the one hand, you want to dissuade persons who are only looking for free items and nothing else, but you also want to attract the highest level of genuine customers. Obviously, if you are only sending electronic information, such as an email, or a download, this won't be as much of an issue, compared to if you were offering a physical product, such as a free sample, which will cost you much more to send. Count the cost before you start promoting a free offer.

Let's look at the pros and cons of different lengths of forms, in connection with free offers. At the short end of the scale, an online form may be as simple as simply asking for an email address. This will probably generate the most enquiries, as it is the most simple and quick to complete and submit. If you set up an auto-responder, which is highly recommended in such circumstances, the enquiries can be handled "behind the scenes," which is a more efficient way of handling the data. If you are not sure what an auto-responder does, or how to set one up, type the term into a search engine such as www.google.com, and you will find all the information you need. When used correctly, auto-responders not only save you time in responding personally to each enquiry, but they can also filter out genuine enquiries from time wasters, so they are a valuable tool.

At the other end of the scale, some online forms ask for the full address and personal information of the visitor, the types of products or services that they are interested in, how they came across the website, and so on. Generally, the longer the form, the easier it is to gauge which enquiries are serious. Also, the more information you have about the customer, the easier it will be to tailor what you provide to their interests and needs.

There are no hard and fast rules on this, but by testing various lengths and styles of forms, you will be able to arrive at the optimum level of serious enquiries.

2

Make Them Pay!

◆

The benefits of outsourcing costs to customers

How would you like to save substantial costs, undercut your competitors, and therefore attract more customers? You can. While this is not a direct marketing method, the result of applying it will be more people buying your product or service, so it can be thought of as an indirect marketing technique.

Greek born entrepreneur Stelios Haji-Ioannou, has rapidly developed an amazing portfolio of companies under the "easy" brand. His first venture, "easy-Internetcafé" now has branches throughout Europe, and a colossal outlet in the heart of *Times Square* in New York City. A successful low-cost airline "easyJet" followed, along with easyCar, easyCinema, easyDorm and easyCruise to name but a few.

The main benefit of each business that is introduced under the "easy" banner, is that consumers gain considerable savings when compared to alternative goods or services. As their founder Stelios puts it, "Our aim is to lower the cost of living." How can they do it? In essence, they explore the marketplace, to determine where the main costs of providing a particular product or service lie.

In the example of the car rental market, they identified that cleaning a vehicle after it is returned is a costly and inefficient aspect of the business. Even where automated car wash machines are used as part of the process, it is still necessary to have someone drive the car through the facility, not to mention the time it takes to manually clean the inside too.

Think "Outside the Box"

Thinking differently from convention, easyCar ask their customers to return the car clean! In fact, it is a requirement that is clearly sign-written on the side of the vehicle! The wording in the rental agreement is along the lines of: *"if you choose not to bring your car back clean, easyCar will perform this task on your behalf and apply a £10 charge."* According to the company, approximately 85% of their customers do bring the car back clean, and presumably the rest are happy to pay the extra charge to have someone else do it for them.

The "bring the car back clean" policy is just one initiative that has saved substantial costs for easyCar. Another way they have reduced costs, is to endeavour to operate just one type of car at each rental location. They have chosen smaller than average (but comfortable) and reliable vehicles, again passing on the savings from the reduced operating costs. Imagine how simplified their paperwork and scheduling is as a result of having a fleet of identical vehicles. Maintenance and repair costs are slashed, and perhaps the best part for their employees is that they no longer have to haggle with customers over the perpetual question, "I thought I was entitled to an upgrade!"

Another example of outsourcing costs to customers can be seen in the many budget airlines that have prospered during the difficult economic period of recent years. While in-flight meals were considered standard at one time, some airlines began to realise that providing meals made up a reasonable chunk of their operating costs. As a result of this realisation, a few airlines stopped serving meals altogether on their flights. However, a more balanced approach of offering meals for a nominal charge seems to be more commonplace. A number of mainstream carriers followed suit, and also outsourced the cost of meals to their customers.

The interesting thing about outsourcing meal costs to the passenger is that on the most part, travellers have reacted remarkably well to the change. The dire financial situation of many airlines was well publicised, so perhaps an awareness of the critical need to cut costs has helped. Indeed, after the terrorist events of September 11th 2001, there was a significant drop in passenger revenue for a sustained period, as well as a requirement for massive investment in new security measures. Whatever the reasoning behind the decision, this example proves that sometimes customers are willing to pay separately for items that were previously included.

Applying the principles to your business:

easyCar outsourced one of their key costs to their customers, and as a result are generally able to offer a much cheaper price, compared to rival car rental firms.

This attracts more customers as a result because everyone appreciates getting a good deal.

If you are in a particularly competitive industry, outsourcing some costs to your customers may make all the difference. It may seem like a contradiction to talk about asking customers to pay for an element of your costs, expecting them to be happy about that, but it really comes down to WHAT costs you outsource and HOW it is done.

How a Small Hotel Attracted Customers

As an example of how this principle might work in a small business, consider an independent, family run hotel. They may not be able to afford to provide a regular shuttle bus service, to and from the local airport or train/bus station. It may be possible however, to provide such a service by outsourcing the cost to the customer.

Staying in a very small, rural hotel near Glasgow (Scotland) on one occasion, I found myself in a similar situation to the one just described. I was without transportation as I had flown in from London. The taxi service proved to be unreliable, as well as time consuming and costly, so I asked the owner of the hotel if I could pay them to drive me to my meeting. They kindly agreed and I suggested that they might consider offering such a service on an official basis, as there was clearly a need. I explained how they might promote it, so that their guests didn't feel as if it was a money making exercise, which it was not.

I didn't think too much more about the advice until a few months later, when I happened to be checking the website of the same hotel. I was delighted to see a number of positive comments from guests, who had since benefited from the simple shuttle service that had been implemented after my last visit.

Whereas in the past, some guests may not have felt inclined to return to the hotel because of the poor transportation links, it was clear that after the owners of the hotel had implemented the new arrangement, guests were delighted, and felt far more inclined to return over and over to the delightful, but isolated location. They knew that a low-cost, convenient transportation option was now available.

How an Entertainer Increased his Bookings

Let's consider another example. As a marketing consultant within the entertainment industry, I was approached by an entertainer, who we'll call Frank. Frank worked in the corporate sector of show-business, entertaining at company functions and parties. I knew that he did a great job, but he bemoaned the fact that he had not been winning many contracts of late. Frank knew that his fees were competitive, yet potential clients kept turning him down and his core business was dwindling.

I knew there must have been a simple reason why this was happening, so I investigated further. I asked Frank how he had worked out his pricing. How exactly had he structured his quotes? As a result of this examination, it transpired that Frank had been including transport and accommodation costs as part of his quotation, and because he was not shopping around to get a good deal on these costs, his overall quotes were disproportionately high. They had been adversely affected by these subsidiary costs, which he was not even making a profit on, anyway.

The solution seemed fairly obvious and, thankfully, Frank could see the logic behind my recommendation. The answer was to outsource the additional costs to the client. How? When preparing quotations, he stated the performance fee alone, whilst adding a simple note, along the lines of: *"Transportation and Accommodation costs to be covered by client."* This simple adjustment meant less work for Frank in preparing quotes, so he saved time (and was happy about that), and because his quotations were much lower in price, he won a lot more business as a result.

Incidentally, if you are thinking that it is underhanded not to include travel and accommodation costs in a quote of this nature, think again. In Frank's case, the reality was that in most instances, the clients got a better deal, because the vast majority of companies have an in-house travel desk, or at the very least, easy access to competitive prices on airfares and hotels. Most companies actually *prefer* to book these kinds of costs themselves as they feel more in control, and they can more easily claim the expense against tax.

On the rare occasions when companies do ask Frank to make his own travel arrangements, he now has a list of Internet sites where he knows he will get a good deal. Although it's still not his own money (he is reimbursed by the client), companies know that Frank has shopped around for a fair price, and they appreciate that. It's a subtle way of demonstrating that he has their best interests at heart, and they are far more inclined to use Frank for their future entertainment needs, in preference to other performers that they do not know or trust.

Be Honest and Upfront

As a final word of caution on this point, since you will be asking customers to pay for something extra, it is very important that they are kept well informed about what is required of them. This is especially true if what you are asking is a departure from what they are used to, as in the example of easyCar.

As noted earlier, easyCar makes sure that the customer understands the requirement to bring the car back clean. There is no small print, hidden clauses to catch customers out, or any other unconventional tactics to disguise it. In fact, easyCar used this requirement in a positive way as a USP (unique selling point)—yes, as a marketing tool. They reassured customers that they will be getting a better deal as a result of not having to pay the high cleaning costs that other companies have to incorporate into their rates. It appears that most people are more than happy to keep the car clean, knowing that they are getting a great price because of that.

In your own business, think carefully, ask yourself if there are any costs that could be outsourced to the customer. A detailed examination of your business may well reveal some surprises in this regard. Remember though to make all such charges transparent, and ensure that the customer sees a benefit. You certainly don't want them to feel cheated, you want them to be confident in the knowledge that they are getting a great deal.

3

Keep Customers Well Informed

◆

Gaining the most value from every customer

Businesses often make reference to their "customer acquisition cost," which is simply a calculation of the amount of money that has to be spent, in order to attract each paying customer. It's an average amount, which is determined by first adding up how much has been spent on all aspects of marketing within a given period, and then dividing that figure by the total number of customers that are acquired in the same period as a result of marketing.

As an example, let's imagine that you spent $1100 on marketing within a 3 month period, and in the same period you attracted 40 new customers. Your customer acquisition cost would be 1100 divided by 40, which is 27.5, so each customer has been "bought" for a price of $27.50. It follows that you need to make at least $27.50 back from each customer before you start to profit from them.

Is it really necessary to get bogged down with such details? Yes! Working out your customer acquisition cost will reinforce to you just how valuable customers are. The tendency is to forget how much it costs you to get those customers in the first place, and now that you have seen some example figures (I encourage you to work out your own), you will no doubt be more determined to hang on to your valued consumers.

You should also be able to see that it makes more sense to sell to existing customers rather than to ignore them, and continually advertise for new ones. To abandon your current customers is madness; you've already "paid" for them! You should also want your customers to *keep* buying from you, over and over again.

Learning from Amazon.com

One company that understands the importance of this principle is Amazon.com. Once you have placed an order with them for the first time, they make it super easy to place further orders in the future. They make recommendations based on your specific interests, they offer a one click shopping experience to simplify the ordering process, and they send you free shipping offers, discounts, promotions, and so on. All of these techniques work well to keep customers coming back again and again.

Applying the principles to your business:

How can *you* sell to existing customers over and over again? One of the simplest ways is to *keep them informed*. If they have bought something from you once, they are very likely to buy from you again. This means that you have an ongoing responsibility to let them know what you can offer them. If you introduce new products, let them know. If you have special offers, let them know. If you want them to evaluate a product, let them know. It really is that simple, but very few companies do this. Yes, it requires that you keep an accurate database of customers, but with software such as *"Act!"* by Symantec, this is now very simple.

E-mail is currently the most effective tool for keeping in contact with customers, for a number of reasons. Firstly it is ultra cheap—no printing, no envelopes, no stamps, and so on. Secondly, it is quick. Within a few minutes, you can notify your customers of a special offer. Thirdly, you can direct them to an order page on your website with one click, which means many people will buy on impulse, because you have made it easy for them.

Don't forget that you need to ask your customers permission to send them such emails. If you phrase it in the right way, you will have no problem. If *you* were invited to benefit from exclusive special offers from a company that you had already received a good deal from, and were assured that your email address would not be passed on to a third party, wouldn't you agree to receive such email offers? I would. In fact I do.

The Power of E-mail

Being a real sucker for gadgets and all things technical, on one occasion I bought a couple of items from a website that specialised in such products. I agreed to receive future promotions and offers, and sure enough a week or two later I received a colourful email, which included photographs of about nine new products. A couple of the items appealed, and I also spotted a gadget which I was sure a friend of mine would be interested in, so I forwarded the email to him along with a brief note. So out of that simple email notification to one customer, what did the company get? Another two orders! What did it cost them? Nothing but a bit of time to write the email! Multiply the effect over thousands of emails, and you can surely see the potential.

E-mail really is an easy way to increase your sales, simply by notifying current customers that you still exist, and that you have some items they may be interested in.

If you don't know how to setup or send emails, get someone else to do if for you, or learn it. It's a small investment that will pay off almost immediately. There are many good software programs that automate the task for you. Search for "bulk email senders." Remember, it's not spam because you are only emailing individuals who have agreed to receive information from you. Spam is defined as email messages that are sent indiscriminately, which is pointless, not to say illegal in many parts of the world. Make sure you understand the difference otherwise you could end up on the wrong side of the law.

Although email is probably the preferred method of communication for the reasons cited earlier, there is nothing to stop you sending your marketing information via fax or regular mail. Depending on your type of business, those methods may be superior, it just depends. For example, if you know that very few of your customers are likely to have a computer or email access, there is little point using that method, and it may be better to send them a flyer or postcard in the post. Both of these are effective and inexpensive alternatives.

Whatever method of communication you use, make sure it is friendly. Don't come across as a faceless multinational corporation (even if you are). People buy from people they like and trust. Be honest and conversational in your communication, like a conversation with a friend. Customers relate to that, and they appreciate it.

In time, you will look back and remember the times when you used to place ads indiscriminately—here, there, and everywhere, just to keep the flow of customers running. What a waste of money that was, when your most loyal customers were ready and willing to keep on spending with you!

4

Handling Complaints

✦

Turning complainers into loyal customers

In the summer of 2003, British Airways check-in staff at Heathrow airport suddenly staged a mass walk-out over a dispute about working conditions. It appears that they were deeply unhappy about a management decision to introduce a new electronic system, for clocking in and out of work.

The effect of the strike on travellers was disastrous. Over a period of about three days, more than 80,000 passengers suffered cancellations, as a result of 360 flights being cancelled. Only a handful of the scheduled flights took off, and the backlog of travellers from the strike period meant that marquees had to be erected outside the airport, to house all the people who had assumed they would be leaving the country for their summer holidays. The whole situation was chaos, and the resulting negative media coverage only served to do damage to the airlines reputation.

British Airways had to do something, and although they could never make up for the inconvenience caused, they did whatever they could to get passengers off on their journeys as soon as possible. Then they proceeded to rectify the unhappiness within their own ranks.

When it was clear that the situation had calmed down, and an agreement had been reached with their staff, the airline made a sensible move. They contacted all of their frequent travellers via email or regular mail, and apologised for what had happened (in truth they had already done this, but another apology certainly didn't hurt). However, actions speak louder than words as the saying goes, and B.A. implemented a special four day sale, a "Saying Sorry Sale" as they called it. Slashing prices on many popular routes, they gave loyal customers the opportunity to grab a real bargain.

The sale had the desired effect. Bookings were jump started, and confidence in the airline headed back in the right direction, after the earlier severe knock. Many customers who had been left with a bad taste in their mouth were appeased, and the business gradually turned around.

A Dwindling Mobile Phone Company Surges Back to Life

Another company that suffered in its early days was the UK mobile phone operator, One2One. Whilst the prices and customer service were both good, the infrastructure of the network was letting them down badly, to the point that they began losing customers rapidly. Word quickly spread that One2One phones had a very poor reception, and because most people knew signal strength was fundamental to a choice of operator, the knock on effect was disastrous.

The reality was that the expansion of the One2One network was well under way, and the company knew that if customers waited a little while longer, they would benefit from a superior network, compared to some of the other operators who were more popular at the time. As it happened, some of the competing networks were struggling. Why? They had too many customers compared to the capacity of the networks, which resulted in many missed or dropped calls.

One2One were still plagued with being branded as the network with the worst reception however, and they realised that this would be a very difficult label to shake off. What did they do? They changed their name.

In 2001, One2One announced that they would change their name to T-mobile, the mobile brand of its parent form, Deutsche Telekom. Interestingly, another leading company, BT Cellnet also changed its name at the same time to O_2, and the resulting confusion meant that most people had no idea of which company was which. The old perceptions of network problems became a thing of the past and T-Mobile were able to regain a substantial share of the market.

Applying the principles to your business:

If you mess up in a way that affects customers adversely, admit it, and do something immediately to make amends. How might you mess up? You might overcharge someone without realising it; a service may not be completed within the agreed timescale, and so on. There are many possibilities, but the point is not to leave your customers in an unhappy state. A disgruntled, badly treated customer has the potential to do a lot of damage to a small business, because they will talk to their friends, and those friends will tell their friends, and so on. Bad news spreads like wildfire, and you may find yourself pr your company struggling to overcome a tarnished reputation.

Be honest when there are delivery issues or other challenges, and if you make a mistake with an order, make up for it by compensating in some way. All these things go a long way in developing a strong, long lasting relationship with your customers.

Let's look at the positive side of complaints. There's a positive side? Yes, there is. If you handle an unhappy customer in the right way, by calmly listening to their complaint and taking appropriate action, you have the real possibility of turning them around to the point where they actually become more loyal than they were before. That might sound strange, but it's true. Exactly what you do to satisfy an unhappy customer depends on a number of factors, including how much they have spent, how long they have been a customer, and whether or not they have already requested something specific in the way of compensation. Discretion is required as no two situations will be alike.

Customer Service in the Airline Industry

Let's take another airline example, but this time it involves a personal experience. On a set of internal flights in the USA, I experienced a number of problems, with a flight cancellation and lost luggage being the most frustrating. The seeming incompetence of the airline caused great inconvenience.

Local staff on the ground did not prove to be very helpful in coming to my aid, or even in attempting to rectify the situation, so on returning home I wrote to the customer service department of the airline. To be honest, I was not expecting much in the way of a reply. However, I was annoyed about the way I had been treated and I wanted to bring the matter to their attention. In truth, I had already decided in my own mind that I would not use the airline again.

The response that came back however, was a great surprise. Firstly, it was quick, which is always a shock. How many times have you found yourself writing a complaint letter to a company, only to forget about it until three months later, when a standard issue letter pops through your letter box? In the case I just referred to, the letter I received was not a generic letter of the "insert name here" variety (do companies really expect us to feel anything other than disgust at those letters)? Also, my specific concerns and frustrations had been individually addressed in the reply, with reasons given as to why problems had occurred, and promises that further action would be taken to avoid them happening again. Wow. You can imagine my surprise, but there is more. The airline made a generous offer of compensation, which I knew they were under no obligation to do.

As a result of this communication, the airline retained a regular customer, as I felt reassured that my business was valued. Although I had previously decided not to use them again, the way they handled my complaint restored my confidence, and I am pleased to say that I have only had positive experiences with them since.

There is a powerful lesson here. Even when things go wrong (which they will do), your response should involve a prompt, active marketing effort, to win the customer back again. Marketing? What kind of marketing? Remind the customer that you view them as valuable, and provide plenty of reasons why they should stay with you. Remember, their confidence and trust has taken a knock. You need to remind them, even "re-sell" them on why they should continue to do business with you, yes even offering compensation if necessary. It's a small price to pay in the long run.

5

Dare to be Different

✦

*How to grab the attention
of prospective customers*

From an early age, even as a baby, we are conditioned to mimic others. That "programming" seems to stay with us throughout our lives because generally, most people follow the crowd. Look at fashion for example. We virtually become slaves to it, by conforming to the same styles that we see recommended by others. If you don't believe that, simply take a look back at your old photo albums. You will be able to tell at a glance whether specific photos were taken during the 60's, 70's, 80's or 90's, just by looking at the clothes you were wearing at the time!

In business too, most people follow the crowd. Few dare to be different, but it's those that do that tend to reap the greatest rewards.

Master Magician's Magical Marketing

Working with the magician Paul Daniels, who has had an incredible career, performing more magic on TV than any other magician in history, has been a delight for me, because we both see eye to eye when it comes to marketing. Despite the substantial age difference between us, Paul believes, as do I, that in order to truly stand out from the crowd, you need to do something radically different from the norm, something different from what people *expect*. Paul likes to challenge convention, because invariably it gets him noticed, and in the business of entertainment, that is his aim!

On one occasion, Paul was due to perform shows during the entire month of Scotland's Edinburgh Festival. We had been finding that advertising posters were just not cutting it in terms of attracting people to book seats for Paul's shows, so we had to look at alternatives. Just to prove the point about posters, when Paul was booked to perform at a theatre in a town in the north of England, the morning of the show he decided to have a haircut in a salon located directly opposite the theatre. Having been shown to a seat by the window, the girl cutting his hair asked Paul why he was in town. He simply pointed out of the window across to the theatre on the other side of the road, which was literally covered from top to bottom in posters advertising Paul's show! That experience was by no means isolated and it seemed to prove the point that posters are not as effective as they used to be.

There is a Chinese proverb that says, "There is no scenery in familiarity." Think about that. We are so used to our surroundings that our visual sense often goes into an autopilot mode, and we fail to see the "scenery," the interesting things all around us that first time visitors would notice.

Paul tends to "firkle ideas in his head" as he calls it, which basically means he observes things on his travels that could be used for marketing, stores them away, and they usually resurface later in a useable format. Indeed, the brain is more wonderful than any computer. So in relation to the Edinburgh festival, one of the many ideas that Paul came up with was to buy and refurbish an old quadra-cycle bike (the type that are sometimes available for hire in seaside resorts). These quadra-cycles are four wheeled bicycles that can accommodate two or three passengers—the two on the outside pedal the bike, and one of them steers. This kind of bike is so unusual that we were sure it would be noticed.

Paul managed to track down one of these bikes, but it was in a sorry state, and needed a complete overhaul. Still, he bought it for a bargain, and my father-in-law who is a special effects whiz in the film industry (he was responsible for building and operating R2-D2 in Star Wars) took up the challenge. A few weeks later, the refurbished bike was unveiled, and it looked like new, with a shiny red paint job, as well as fantastic advertising banners across the top of the canopy. Needless to say, Paul caused a real stir when he rode this contraption around Edinburgh. It became a talking point amongst visitors and locals alike, and outstanding media coverage was given for the show. As a result, sales skyrocketed after that.

Occasionally large corporations have been known to try unconventional marketing, and IBM, the computer and software giant is an interesting example to consider.

IBM wanted to promote the LINUX operating system, so they employed graffiti artists to paint pavements and walls in various cities with the phrase 'Peace, Love, and Linux.' Incidentally, they were careful to use bio-degradable chalk.

The message got noticed, the news media picked up on it, and the resulting national news coverage was invaluable.

Times Square in New York is well known for its high concentration of billboards, posters, and advertising. Many of those colourful displays cost a small fortune, and yet on one occasion that I visited that area, it was something completely different that caught, and held my attention.

Some enterprising person had arranged for dogs to carry promotional messages in little pouches on their backs. This was clever, because the people that thought of the idea used small dogs of unusual breeds that caught the attention of passers-by. Each dog had a handler with them, and together, in four or five 'teams' they roamed Times Square. Exploiting a natural human trait, members of the public would notice these unusual dogs, get stopped in their tracks, crouching down to 'say hello' to the dog, patting it etc. The handler would then present the dog lover with a leaflet for a particular product, normally related to pets in some way, such as a promotion for a brand of pet food.

Companies using this advertising method were paying hundreds of dollars for each dog, each day, and were delighted with the results!

A TV Commercial that Broke the Mould

When watching the TV and the commercials come on, most people make a drink, take a trip to the bathroom, or carry out some other task. Advertisers have therefore had to be increasingly clever to attract and hold the attention of viewers. This also applies to other forms of advertising such as billboards, posters, radio commercials and so on. There is an endless quest to come up with adverts that motivate consumers to buy.

An interesting example of creative advertising can be seen in the marketing efforts of the cruise company, Royal Caribbean International. For years, their TV commercials had featured ships. That seems fairly reasonable on face value, but consumers get bored very easily, and RCI were also trying to overcome certain stereotypes about the cruise industry.

When RCI came to the realisation that it was not necessary to show the actual product (the ship), their advertising suddenly became fresh, innovative, even inspiring. In fact, it worked a treat—so much so that they were awarded first place in an industry vote for the best advertising of the year.

In case you were wondering what RCI showed in place of ships, they focused on the excitement of the ports of call and the general adventure element of a cruise. The ads were filmed in a modern, upbeat style and viewers felt good whilst watching them. The strap line was "Get out there"—the message being that you can have a lot of fun on a cruise ship vacation. You are not stuck on the ship; rather you have plenty of opportunities to explore fascinating places, and take part in exhilarating activities like snorkelling, diving, rock climbing, and so on.

This fresh approach also appealed to a younger generation of first time cruisers, a lucrative market that was opening up. To this group, cruising had previously been perceived as boring, and only for the elderly, but this stereotype was cleverly overcome by the groundbreaking TV commercials.

Applying the principles to your business:

However tempting it may be (and it *is* very tempting), marketing is one aspect of business where it's *not* good to follow the crowd. In order to be most effective, your marketing must be special, unusual, not conforming to what you see everyone else doing. It should make people sit up and take notice; you must dare to be different.

In planning a fresh approach to your advertising, ask yourself, what effect does the product or service have on the one using it? What are the *benefits* to the customer by using it? Is there a parallel in another industry that you could learn from or refer to? Could comedy be used to reinforce important points? Could an ongoing story be developed that unfolds over a period of time in a series of adverts?

Bear in mind that the need for creativity applies to any form of marketing. Whether you are sending out a brochure or a sales letter, handing out a business card, or even when talking to someone about your business, strive to be creative in your approach. Make sure the customer will remember you.

A wedding photographer by the name of Ramon, approached me to help him promote his service. On examining the marketplace, it turned out that the majority of his competitors would send out a brochure and price list to prospective clients. If Ramon had done the same, there would be little to set him apart from the other photographers.

The solution we devised was to produce a dynamic presentation on CDROM, which played in any computer or DVD player. The disc featured a thorough explanation of the benefits of the service, as well as examples of Ramon's work, all set to a moving soundtrack. Anyone viewing this presentation could not help but be moved by the striking content; it was emotionally powerful, and uplifting at the same time. At the end of the presentation, the viewer also had the option of clicking a link to Ramon's website, for even more information.

It's worth noting that this method of promotion, worked out cheaper than producing full colour brochures, *and* it was highly effective.

On a visit to San Francisco, I noticed one evening that there was a music event happening in the city, at one of the large auditoriums. There must have been around eight to ten thousand people lined up around the block and into the distance, just waiting for the doors to open.

A local radio station had hit upon the idea of projecting a 60' high image on to the side of a brick wall of an adjacent building, in clear view of the crowds of concert-goers! The projection was a simple image promoting the radio station.

This was an ingenious idea, because the advert was in full view of virtually every single person waiting for the concert, and everyone would have noticed and taken in the message of the huge image.

Incidentally, you may be thinking that such a 'stunt' would have cost a lot of money. At the time I was intrigued as to how it was achieved, so I investigated further. A block or so away from where the image could be seen, there were a couple of lads with an LCD projector, some crates, and bungee rope to secure it! The projector could have been hired for around £30 ($50) for the evening, the image was probably designed by one of the students, and stored as a 'freeze frame' in the projector, and the crates were probably borrowed from a nearby bar!

Remember, that promotional message was seen by about 10,000 people. Now that's cheap advertising!

Note that when you dare to be different, people will naturally talk to each other about what they have seen, and word of mouth spreads quickly. Typically you'll hear people say something like, "Guess what I saw/heard/received today?" That is very powerful publicity!

Business cards are a common method of marketing a business, but again, think about how you can develop a card that will stand out as different.

Next time you get a batch of business cards printed, you could ask the printer to punch a small hole in the corner of every one. It costs a little extra, but you can use this unusual technique to help people remember you. After all, how many times have you been given a business card that had a hole in it? Incidentally, if you don't want to pay the extra, buy a hole punch and do a few at a time yourself.

When someone asks you why the hole is there, you could say "When you look at the card again in a few days, it will remind you that *you must look into it!*"

Or you could simply say "It's so that you remember me as the painter/plumber/insurance salesman with the hole in his business card."

As an extension of this type of idea, why not get your business cards cut into an unusual shape? You may not realise it, but printers can cut all kinds of shapes, you only have to ask. Again, it will make you stand out from the crowd, because most people use a standard, rectangular shaped card.

You might also consider using credit-card style plastic cards, with your details etched on them. Again, very few people are using these, yet they are inexpensive and most people will hold on to them, because they have a high perceived value.

As a young man, Paul Daniels, the entertainer referred to earlier, once worked in local government, and he bought stationery for his entire office. One day, a man came in offering a line of stationery products. He explained that it was his own business, and gave Paul a business card which was actually a tiny card, about an inch square. Intrigued by this, Paul enquired, "Why is it so small?" The man replied, "Well, it's got my name and number, that's all the information you need, and it all fits neatly on that size of card!"

After the man left, Paul showed the little business card to everyone in the office because it was so unusual. The problem however, was that there were strict rules governing who Paul could buy stationery products from, and he doubted whether he would be able to use the guy with the small business card.

Some months passed, until on one occasion, Paul needed some supplies very urgently, and none of the usual suppliers could help. Immediately, the 'man with the small card' came to mind. Paul found the little card, called the man, and was quoted a good price for the goods. Amazingly, the entire order was delivered within two hours!

Needless to say, Paul was impressed. What's more, the next day in the mail, a large A4 (legal size) envelope landed on Paul's desk. Thinking it was an invoice, Paul slid the contents out and found it to be a huge business card, the same size as the envelope! Attached to the card was a note that read, "Thank you for your order…I can now afford a proper business card!" Paul never bought supplies from anyone else after that! Again, another example of someone who dared to be different, and it worked amazingly well.

Whatever advertising concept you come up with, there are some general rules that you should always follow. You need to laser target your marketing precisely to the audience that you want to appeal to. Remember, the smaller the niche, the better. General advertising that tries to encompass the whole population is rarely effective.

When I meet clients for the first time and ask them who their product or service is aimed at, often the same answer comes back, "everyone." That's not good enough. You *must* narrow it down. At the very least, your target audience should be defined as something like "males, aged 18 to 35" or "children from 5 to 10 years old." Better still would be "left handed golfers" or "catering managers in 5 star hotels," or "out of work actors in the South-East region." Do you get the idea? Try and appeal to a specific group of people according to your pre-determined criteria of who is most likely to buy what you are offering.

6

Give Customers What They Want

✦

Fulfilling customer's needs to boost sales

In modern times, cinemas have not changed much in the way they operate. Most towns have a large, multi-screen complex, showing first-run films, and they usually make massive profits from selling overpriced hotdogs, popcorn, soft drinks etc. Stelios from the easy group of companies looked at the way the current major cinema chains (such as UCI, Warner Brothers, and Showcase) operated in the UK, and he decided to challenge convention.

After some initial research, Stelios felt sure that there is a large number of people that primarily go to the cinema purely for *entertainment,* rather than to see a specific film at a specific time. He felt sure that if customers were offered great films at ridiculously low prices, there would be plenty of people who would be interested in viewing those films, even if they were not the current releases. Certainly it was an interesting idea that fits with the marketing principle of giving people what *they* want rather than what *you* want to give them.

Thus, the easyCinema concept was born, and the first multi-screen complex opened in Milton Keynes (UK) in May 2003.

Apart from the changes to the *type* of films that are shown, a number of other changes were introduced. Firstly, there is no staffed ticket office. Tickets must be purchased over the Internet or by phone, or alternatively at stand alone automated kiosks in the lobby of the Cinema, which results in significant savings on operational costs.

Secondly, a brand new and radically different pricing structure for tickets was implemented. As bookings are received, the price for each film increases gradually, even within the same day, according to its popularity. So in simple terms, the more seats that get booked, the higher the price you pay. If you book early, you get a better deal. In real terms, many seats are sold for as little as 20p (U.S. $0.50)! Even the most expensive tickets remain well below the price of competing multiplexes.

The third major change was to scrap the sale of refreshments such as popcorn and drinks etc. Customers are encouraged to bring their own food and beverage items, and are kindly asked to take their litter away when they leave, which brings to mind the easyCar philosophy mentioned earlier.

What was the public reaction to the new cinema? After all, that's what counts. Interestingly, in its first week of operation, easyCinema achieved 56% occupancy in an industry that averages 20%. Since then, the concept has had time to prove itself, and easyCinema looks set to make a profit from low margin, high yield sales of tickets. Because they are filling the cinemas, they can charge a lot less than their competitors and still make a profit. Needless to say, the established cinema chains are not happy.

Richard Branson is another example of someone who holds the philosophy of giving customers what *they* want close to his heart. With every business venture he has undertaken, he consults his family and friends to seek their opinion on every detail.

This willingness to listen to "ordinary" customers has paid dividends. For example, seemingly simple changes to the service style aboard Virgin Atlantic aircraft had a dramatic effect on customer satisfaction. Rather than starting with, "this is what we can offer," the Virgin approach was to ask "what do *travellers* really *want*?"

How Nokia Won Mobile Phone Customers

A further example of this is the mobile phone manufacturer Nokia. In a super-competitive marketplace, Nokia cleverly stole a large share of the market at an early stage of the game, by giving customers what they wanted.

In the late 1990's and early into the millennium, Nokia realised that what men and women wanted from cell phones was dramatically different. Men generally wanted lots of features and games, whereas women tended to want a phone that was small, and that looked like a fashion accessory.

Nokia managed to satisfy both groups, by manufacturing technologically advanced phones, with the option of interchangeable covers. This latter feature of being able to personalise a phone with removable covers of every colour and style, proved to be a winning formula for Nokia, and their sales went through the roof when this option was introduced. Note that the success was down to giving customers what *they* wanted, not what the technical people at Nokia thought they should offer.

Applying the principles to your business:

Astonishingly, most businesses do not give their customers what the customers ask for. They persist in offering what THEY want to offer, and as a result, they often lose the sale.

A funny thing happened on one occasion when I went looking for a new car. Having arrived in the dealers parking lot, I walked towards the vehicles that I was interested in, but could only get a short distance before being pounced on by an over eager salesman. You know the type.

Before I could utter a word, the salesman proceeded to list all the features and details of the car I happened to be standing beside. I literally could not get a word in, until finally, when the salesman paused for breath, I said, "Actually, I have no interest in this model, I came to look at the X brand."

Not learning his lesson, the salesman then tried to sell me a particular colour and style of the car that I had expressed an interest in. The problem was, I was not interested in the colour and style of vehicle that the salesman liked.

Can you see what happened? The salesman tried to sell me the cars *he* liked rather than asking me what I was interested in.

In the end I grew so fed up that I went to another dealer, and found a salesman that showed a real interest in helping fulfil my requirements, rather than selling me a particular model that I was not interested in.

With your business, be determined to listen to your customers. Never jump to a conclusion about their needs, always ask them and seek their opinion.

It's also important not to stay with convention or tradition, if you believe that may be wrong. Times change, and what people want often changes with the passing of time. Find out what people want *now*. If no one is offering that, you have a perfect opportunity to plug the gap in the market, just like easyCinema and Nokia did.

Remember, whatever you are selling, find out what people want. Don't assume anything. Ask them! And *keep* on asking them!

7

Go with the Flow, not against it

◆

The importance of keeping up with ever changing trends

Stamp collecting, hula hoops, platform shoes, Barbie dolls, skateboarding, video games, and tattoos are all fads that have appeared over the years. Some stay around longer than others, but in general terms these are a few examples to demonstrate that the world is constantly changing. In the business world, there are many companies that refused to go with the flow, and got left behind. Others adapt and remain profitable.

Both my wife and I love to travel, and therefore it was very interesting to work on a number of projects with British Airways, who are one of the world's largest airlines. The last twenty years has seen some enormous changes in that industry, many of which could never have been predicted, and each change called for a radical rethink of marketing strategies. Let's look back over some of the key changes and see how British Airways reacted.

Until the mid 1980's, it seemed that British Airways had got into a bit of a rut with their advertising. Most of their offerings were fairly bland, and *very* British. But since that time, they have radically changed their approach, and thought carefully about what would appeal to their customers. Each campaign in the last fifteen years or so has been specifically targeted to a much narrower group of customers, sometimes referred to as niche markets.

In the yuppie era of the 1980's, British Airways ad campaigns featured hardworking white collar workers dashing to get on the "red eye" (night time flight) to maximise their working time during daylight hours. At the time, that's what business flying was all about. The innovation of laptop computers meant that employees could take their work with them, and many individuals seemed to be working all the hours in the day. Hollywood movies such as *"Wall Street"* coined phrases like "lunch is for wimps." Most companies were raking in money in the booming economy, and B.A. succeeded in attracting a substantial number of customers in the top end of the business market, where the fares were the highest and the yields the greatest.

Coming into the mid 1990's, there was much more emphasis on "looking after yourself," even to the point of pampering oneself. With many young people suffering from burnout or Chronic Fatigue Syndrome, the trend was to be more sensibly paced, and to reward hard work with equal amounts of "play". B.A. wanted to get the message across that if you flew with them, they would really look after you, and that flying could be a time to relax and unwind, away from the stresses of the office. The "Up on the roof" campaign worked well in conveying this. Using the relaxing musical theme *"Up on the roof,"* the commercial showed an executive relaxing in a swimming pool on the top of a skyscraper within a big city. Two environments were featured at the same time—the workplace, and the relaxation area. This concept fitted well with the intended marketing message and the campaign was a great success.

In the mid 1990's airlines started to form alliances with each other. The first major alliance named the *"Star Alliance"* incorporated Virgin, United, Lufthansa, Singapore Airlines and others. This partnership of airlines meant more benefits to customers, and more sales for the airlines.

British Airways took the initiative to create another major alliance, named "One World," with the emphasis on a smoother travel experience as a result of the cooperation of a number of airlines. A high profile and extended advertising campaign targeted regular travellers, who were most likely to benefit from the new alliance.

In the late 1990's, B.A. realised that the majority of their passengers at that time were not British, which seems rather odd, as it was the predominant national airline. After conducting surveys, they found that many foreigners were keen on the British Airways service style, and were choosing B.A. over their own national airlines. Whereas many British people considered B.A. to be too formal and stuffy, that unique service style was often considered to be a positive aspect by many other nations. It was a challenge to appeal to both types of customer (which they tried for a while), and B.A. were keen to attract more British passengers, so they launched a series of adverts that attempted to draw in more of their national passengers. However, no one could have predicted what was to come next...

In to the year 2000 and beyond, recession was hitting many countries. The boom time of business air travel was definitely over, and many companies cut back on their staff air travel. The events of September 11, 2001 struck another blow to an already ailing industry. This resulted in a massive cutback in air travel by many companies, both from the point of view of saving costs, as well as an element of fear of further terrorist attacks. Many companies chose to use video links rather than send their employees on flights.

At the time, B.A. had to think very carefully about how to try and win back the lucrative business travel sector, and they came up with an award winning marketing concept. The advert showed two UK based businessmen, who were independently trying to win a lucrative contract in the USA. One of them was shown trying to do the deal on the phone, whereas the other flew over to the USA and met personally with the client. The strap line was: *"It's better to be there"*—the notion being that when doing business with other countries, if there is a choice between communicating by phone or email, compared to being there in person, "it's better to be there." The campaign went a long way in helping to rekindle business travel.

Looking back over the years, it is amazing how much companies like B.A. have changed. Although they may not have wanted to go down a certain route with their service, if that's the way the market leads them then at a particular time, it would be foolish to go against the flow. Imagine if British Airways had dug their heels and said, "No, we will offer customers what *we* think is best for them." The business would have died a quick death.

Let's take another example, this time from the world of photography. Since the 1990's, digital cameras have steadily risen in popularity to the point where they overtook the sales of traditional film cameras by a substantial margin. Companies like Kodak and Fuji, whose businesses were focused on manufacturing rolls of film, had to embrace this new digital technology, or be left out in the cold. Although the adoption of digital cameras was a gradual process, it was unrelenting, and it has meant a radical rethink of the business structure of all traditional camera and film manufacturers.

Demonstrating just how far the world of photography has changed, early in 2004, Kodak announced that they would no longer be selling traditional film cameras in western markets, such as the U.S.A., Canada and Western Europe.

Applying the principles to your business:

We have seen that as the years pass by, consumer trends vary dramatically. What suits buyers at one particular time may change very quickly. It is essential to keep up to date with what your customers want. You should constantly be re-evaluating the marketplace. What are your customer's *current* needs? Have world events had an impact on what they want? Has new technology affected their view of your products or services? Should you consider developing and offering other products or services that better fit changing needs? Has new competition opened up which could threaten to take a share of the market you are in?

How can you tell what changes are happening? There are several things you can, and should do. Keep up to date with the news—every day if possible. Ask your customers directly how you can serve them better. You may well be surprised at how helpful they are. Observe people everywhere. Are new trends emerging in what they wear, what they eat, their choice of music and entertainment, and so on? All these things are indicators of trends.

To be effective in business, you really need to be one step ahead all the time, pre-empting the changes that are likely to affect your business. For example, nowadays the market is swamped with products that relate to diets, keeping fit, and so on. It's probably too late to cash in on those trends because so many companies got their first. Imagine if you had been aware of massive growth areas like the use of computers, the Internet, digital cameras, and the introduction of CD's and DVD's for example. Knowing what you know now about these things, would you have liked knowledge of them *before* they exploded in a big way? There will be just as many similar sized developments in the future...

8

Joint Ventures

◆

How to harness the enormous potential of business link-ups

Joint ventures are definitely in vogue, and for good reason. When the right partnerships are made, both companies benefit by making more profit, and the customer often perceives that they are getting added value.

These link-ups can take many forms of course. Sometimes it is an agreement to recommend a product or service of another company, such as in the case of commercials for washing machines, where they say might something like, "for best results, we recommend the use of XYZ brand of washing powder." Was that recommendation made out of the kindness of their hearts? Of course not. Advertising air time on TV costs a fortune, and there is no way that companies would recommend something if there was no benefit to doing so. Similarly, the washing powder company will reciprocate by recommending a specific appliance manufacturer "for the best possible clean." They also do deals, so that, for example, with every washing machine sold, the detergent company "donates" a sample of its product to use in the machine. The hope is that their subtle ploy moves the customer to stay with that brand in the future.

Such recommendations are highly effective of course, the reason being that the customer already has a relationship and trust of company "A," so when company "A" suggests that the consumer tries the products or services of company "B," the consumer has confidence in that recommendation, and invariably they will accept the advice.

Another type of joint venture is where two or more companies cooperate to sell, (rather than simply promote) each others product or services. An example where this has worked well is the Disney and McDonalds link up. This is a relationship that has grown much stronger over the last five years or so. The nature of the link up of these two companies is simple. Both companies know that their main target audience is made up of kids—not exclusively, but they certainly make up the majority of their customers.

You have probably noticed that whenever Disney release a major new movie, McDonalds features toys, goodies and sometimes even themed meals that relate to the film. At the same time, Disney advertises the film and promotes the special items that are only available through McDonalds. Disney are pleased because they are getting massive publicity for their film through every McDonalds outlet in the country, and McDonalds are happy because many more customers are being driven into their stores, as a result of the Disney advertising.

Barnes & Noble Join Forces with Starbucks

Another successful link up is the partnership of Barnes and Noble bookstores and Starbucks Coffee shops. Across the USA, the more than 400 Barnes & Noble outlets feature a Starbucks outlet within the bookstore. Barnes and Noble are now able to promote themselves as neighbourhood book stores, where customers can sip coffee, mill around, and choose books in a relaxing, comfortable atmosphere. By the time the agreement was made between the two companies, Starbucks was a nationally recognised brand with their own loyal clientele, so offering Starbucks coffee within the bookstores was virtually guaranteed to be successful.

In a similar way, Starbucks also helped Barnes & Noble grow into the company it is today. For example, in the early 1990's, every time Starbucks introduced a new product, a Barnes & Noble coupon was given away to their customers. The two companies also cooperated with joint advertising campaigns that promoted both brands.

Starbucks have arranged joint venture deals with other companies too. In the year 2000 they announced that *The Times* newspaper would be the only national newspaper available in their 3,000 or so American coffee stores at the time. In exchange, Starbucks received premium ad placement in the newspaper.

Applying the principles to your business:

Bearing in mind the type of products or services that you currently offer your customers as part of your business, think about what *other* products or services might appeal to them. You are far more likely to succeed in joint cooperation ventures if you find a good match. This is important, because if you fail to do this, consumers may feel that the recommendation is contrived, and subsequently lose confidence in your company.

Finding a Good Match

How do you find a suitable match? Let's imagine you are a travel agent, selling holidays, flights, car hire and so on. What sort of companies could you link up with, either to recommend their products, or to sell them directly? How about an insurer that specialises in travel insurance? You might also link up with a publisher that has a range of informative books about various destinations. Along similar lines, how about a company that produces a range of travel guide videos? You might find a finance company that is willing to offer a scheme to help customers spread the cost of paying for their holiday. How about a taxi service that is focused on offering airport runs from your home town? That's just a few examples of a good fit. There are usually many opportunities within any type of business.

In the field of creating websites, a potential joint venture partnership exists between web designers and web hosting companies. Since consumers often have no clue about what or who is good or bad or what to look out for, recommendation is extremely valuable. The web designer can direct customers to the web hosting company, and the hosting company can recommend the web designer. Many times, customers will specifically ask for such recommendations, which is even better, because the companies won't even have to "sell" the service.

Whilst we are on the subject of information technology, it's worth mentioning that the Internet provides phenomenal potential for referrals and recommendations. The most common form is a web link which simply means that someone visiting your website could click on a button that takes them to the website of one of your partners. Sometimes these agreements are established as private business arrangements between the two companies, sometimes they are affiliate schemes where the receiving company pays a fee per visitor or per sale on the website. Sometimes the links are provided free, perhaps without the recipient even knowing. Such linking of websites is a large subject on its own, but it's worth keeping it in mind, because it is potentially very powerful for your business.

So now is the time to think about your own business. Write down a list of associated products and services that you know your customers would (or could) use, either at the same time as, or before or after using your product or service. You can even widen the spectrum of your search even further than that. Think about what your customers do and where they spend their time—that may also provide you with further ideas of suitable partnerships. What age range do your customers fall in to? Are they predominantly male or female, young or old?

When you have identified some potential link ups, don't assume that a particular company would not be interested in working with you. You don't know until you ask, and even if they say no, there are bound to be a number of other companies that offer something similar.

Of course, it's also worth noting that you should not choose just any company that is willing to do a deal with you. That would be short-sighted. They *must* have a good reputation in the marketplace already in order for you to consider them. Otherwise *your* hard earned reputation may be affected if problems arise. Don't be afraid to make detailed enquiries about the company before you sign any deal, especially if you are unsure, or something doesn't seem right. A genuine company will not mind you "probing" a little in order to check them out. You should expect them to do the same with your company too.

Once you have found a suitable company, don't forget to discuss and agree on every detail before you commence. Both parties must agree in writing what is expected of them. All too often, this type of arrangement turns sour because one party expected too much of the other, or assumed certain things that later turned out not to be the case. Don't leave anything to chance, and it may be sensible to consult a lawyer who specialises in such agreements. Also, don't get tied down with a contract that locks you in to an agreement for many years, because you may want, or need to get out of it in a shorter time. It's wise to have a test period first, where both parties can try out the agreement to see if it works for them. Despite your best efforts to prepare and cover every eventuality, it's quite possible that it may not work out for some reason.

Remember too that you don't have to limit yourself to just one such relationship. It may be possible to work joint ventures with a number of companies. Obviously you don't want to divert too much attention away from your own product or service, which should always take priority. Ideally, make *your* sale first, and then introduce the related product or service as an add-on. Don't fall into the trap of giving the associated product a higher profile than your own!

The Nuts and Bolts of Joint Ventures

In practical terms, how does this kind of joint venture relationship work? How do you go about recommending each other's products or services?

There are many ways of doing this, and you need to find what works for you. Some companies simply display each others business cards. A good example of that is a restaurant or bar that carries business cards of a local taxi firm. The owners want to ensure their customers get home safely, especially if they have been drinking a lot of alcohol, so they are happy to promote a local taxi firm. Likewise, when passengers of the taxi company ask the driver to recommend a good bar or restaurant in the vicinity, the driver can recommend the establishment that promotes their taxi service.

In another type of business, it might be appropriate to add the logo of the associated company to your own letterhead and marketing materials. If it is a well known brand, this will also serve to enhance your brand, because the customer makes the psychological connection that both companies must be of the same high standard.

Some well known entertainment theme parks use associations with companies such as soft drinks brands like Pepsi or Coke, as well as airlines, photographic equipment suppliers like Kodak, credit card companies and so on. The logos of these companies are prominently displayed on the brochures and marketing of the theme park, and even within the park itself. In return, the theme park usually purchases these products for a much lower price, and can therefore make greater profits on their sales.

A key advantage of joint ventures for the small business is that both companies can potentially get access to each others database of customers. In an instant, you can obtain a targeted mailing list of customers that are likely to buy your products. In the same way, you would share your database with your joint venture partner. This valuable advantage is often overlooked.

9

Expanding into New Regions

◆

How to steadily grow your business

Even with plenty of phenomenal success stories from businesses that have expanded into new geographic regions, very few small businesses consider it. This is probably due to the perception that it is beyond their capabilities. The thought of setting up the same business in another area or country fills them with fear! It involves stepping outside of their comfort zone, entering into the unknown. Actually, it's quite straightforward. The key to success is in the planning.

In this chapter we'll also consider the danger of becoming too focused on a specific *type* of customer within your current geographical area. With a little adaptation, you could probably open up your business to other groups of buyers. Let's consider both of these aspects of expansion...

Firstly, have you ever considered opening up your business to a new geographic area, even including other countries? Whatever your answer to that question you need to ascertain whether your current business is localised, purely serving the local community. If it is, geographic expansion is not ruled out, you just need to find ways of adapting what you sell in order to appeal to a wider audience.

Some other questions to ask at this stage are: Who are your customers at the moment? When, why and where do they buy? How do you get the products or services to them? Who are your main competitors and how much of the market share do they currently have?

The answers to these questions will give you a good indication of whether it would be feasible or worthwhile to expand into a different area.

Assuming that you consider it worth proceeding, you could establish a franchise operation, where someone else runs the business in return for paying you a fee and ongoing commissions. You might also consider a joint venture, or you could do it yourself, if you are in a position to leave your existing business in the care of someone you trust.

Whatever you decide, it is crucial to test the waters before making any large scale commitments. You need to be sure that the new market will buy from you. Many factors can affect businesses within different geographic areas. Variations in culture, standard of living, amount of free time, the average wage and so on can affect whether your business will succeed.

One of the most obvious success stories that involves widening out into different geographic areas are the American fast food giants such as McDonald's, Burger King, KFC etc. All of these started small. Burger King's humble beginnings can be traced back to the mid 1950's when two guys had the idea to open a simple hamburger restaurant. Their first restaurant opened in Miami, Florida, where they sold 18 cent broiled hamburgers and 18 cent milkshakes. They saw the opportunity for expansion, gradually opened outlets across America, and in 1963 they opened their first international restaurants in Puerto Rico.

By 1967 the company had 274 restaurants, with around 8,000 employees. A rapid worldwide expansion followed, and by the late 1990's the company had more than 10,000 restaurants. Currently they have upwards of 12,000 restaurants across 57 countries and territories. Remember how it all started—with one restaurant in a local community.

Similarly, the original creator of McDonald's restaurants, Ray Kroc, opened his first restaurant in 1955. Nowadays, McDonald's has around 30,000 restaurants in 119 countries, serving 46 million customers each day. It's difficult to comprehend those kinds of numbers, but where did it all start? With one restaurant!

The same kind of story can also be repeated for Kentucky Fried Chicken. A 65 year-old gentleman named Colonel Sanders used his $105 social security money to start the business, and it was far from easy. The now famous Colonel spent two years driving across the United States trying to convince restaurants to buy his chicken recipe. He was sure he had a winning formula and yet he was turned down 1,009 times. When someone gave him the break he had been working for, he never looked back, and opened one restaurant, then another, and another, and so on. Nowadays KFC have outlets in some 80 countries and territories around the world.

As mentioned at the outset of this chapter, the other way to expand is to seek out alternative types of customers that you do not currently serve. For example, whilst managing the magician Paul Daniels, during one of our "think tank" sessions together, we realised that most of the products we were selling were aimed at other magicians. That was fine, and it is a great niche market, but we also realised that there was a much wider market available to us, which was virtually untouched.

As a result, we started to target people who are *interested* in magic but who are not magicians. We designed and marketed some products for this market (simple magic tricks and videos/DVD's), built a website at: www.pauldanielsmagicshop.com, and the products continue to sell well to this day.

Applying the principles to your business:

Expansion often seems daunting at first, but the rewards can be phenomenal. Don't automatically conclude that your business is not right for expansion. On the contrary, set your sights high and have an open mind. Remember, you don't *have* to operate the business in a new territory *yourself*. You could employ someone else to do it, and earn ongoing commissions from their sales. It may also be possible or preferable to sell to the new region remotely, from your existing office.

Also, don't neglect the ongoing opportunities to serve different *types* of customers. It's quite likely that there are a range of people that you don't currently sell to, but who would benefit from your products or services. For example, let's say you run a car valet business, and your customers are made up of private individuals. An obvious area to expand into would be the corporate sector, where they will probably pay more, and require a group of cars in the same location to be cleaned, which would cut down on your time and travel expenses.

To take another real life example, on one occasion I was speaking to the owner of a local men's hairdressing salon, who was bemoaning the fact that business was slow. I was aware that there were four other hairdressing salons within the same town, so it was clear that this guy needed a competitive edge, something to make his shop stand out as special.

On a few occasions when I walked past the shop, I noticed that the owner would sit at his computer, which he had hooked up in one corner of the salon. I spoke to him about this, and he acknowledged that during the quiet times he would check his emails, browse the Internet and so on. I suggested that he formally offer broadband Internet access for customers who are waiting for a haircut (free of charge), or as a service on it's own (for a flat fee per ½ hour). He did this, and as well as having a great new feature for existing customers to benefit from, he was also able to attract a different type of customer—those who just wanted to call in to surf the net or collect emails. The local newspaper ran a feature about his shop for free, and business increased as a result of implementing the simple new strategy.

10

Selling Direct

◆

Using the Internet to cut out the middle man

Before the Internet exploded on to the world scene, the most common way to buy products was at local stores. Most people in the developed world walked or drove their car to the relevant store or mall, browsed and made their selections.

Although mail-order has been around for a long time, mostly in the form of catalogues that customers browse in the comfort of their own home, it was only with the advent of the Internet that selling direct has become a viable alternative for many types of businesses. In fact, it's an area that has seen phenomenal growth, mainly due to the lower costs of conducting business, and the huge number of potential buyers.

The ability to use the Internet to sell direct has transformed the way that many consumers buy. Products as diverse as flight tickets, insurance, prescription drugs, and DVD's are now regularly purchased online by millions of people. It is now easier than ever to research a prospective purchase, read reviews, compare prices and so on, all of which makes it an appealing way to buy products and services.

By selling direct, your small business can benefit in a number of ways. Cutting out the middle man removes costs. Some of the savings can be passed on to the customer, and a portion can be retained, increasing profitability. Also, it is easy to update sales information and introduce new products, even on an hour by hour basis if necessary. Compare that to a catalogue or sales brochure—once it has been printed, it usually has to last for at least a month, often longer.

Perhaps the foremost example of success by selling direct to the customer from the Internet is Amazon.com. First opening as on online book and music store in July 1995, the company never stood still, and whilst it has had it's share of rough times, it eventually grew into a publicly traded, Fortune 500 company.

47

From the customer viewpoint, a number of factors are responsible for the extraordinary success of Amazon.com. Firstly, prices are always competitive. Secondly, the website offers visitors a wealth of helpful information to assist in choosing products, such as independent reviews, the ability to browse sections of a book and so on. Thirdly, it is very easy to navigate and place an order. In addition, orders are generally shipped very quickly, and there is a huge choice of stock.

From the company's viewpoint, they saw an opportunity in offering easy to ship, high margin items that are usually the result of impulse buying on the part of the consumer. They streamlined their operation to reduce costs as much as possible, and implemented processes to make it more efficient than conventional retailers.

Nowadays, Amazon.com features millions of items in categories as diverse as apparel and accessories, electronics, sporting goods, gourmet food, computers, kitchenware and house wares, books, music, DVDs, videos, cameras and photo items, toys, baby items and baby registry, software, computer and video games, cell phones and service, tools and hardware, magazine subscriptions and outdoor living items. In fact, the business has been transformed into a vast, but easy to navigate online shopping mall.

Applying the principles to your business:

Although the news media focused a great deal on the so called "dot-bombs" in the past, that is companies that failed to make a success of doing business on the Internet, the reality is that countless companies are profitable, by using the Internet to sell direct to the end user. Where many companies failed is in not understanding the true nature of e-commerce, and they tried to expand too rapidly, which resulted in costs spiralling out of control.

In the early days of the Internet, the costs involved in setting up a business were ridiculous, and it was a difficult, specialised task. Technology has brought many advances in that area, and nowadays it is inexpensive and straightforward, which is great news for you and your business.

A Step by Step Approach to get You Started

If you would like to take your business online, the first step is to research other websites that offer a similar product or service. Determine which ones you like and dislike, and determine the reasons why. Ask friends, relatives, and existing customers what they look for in the type of website you are planning.

The next stage is to obtain a domain name, which is also sometimes known as a website address, usually in the form of "www.companynamehere.com." Many Internet sites (such as www.register.com) can help you set this up.

If you have some computer knowledge, you may wish to design your own site, using software such as *Microsoft FrontPage* or *Macromedia Dreamweaver*. Alternatively, you could ask around to see if anyone can recommend a web designer locally. Bear in mind that whilst a designer will have a good grasp of making the site easy to navigate and visually appealing, YOU should take the responsibility for the content, including the marketing aspects. Wherever possible you should provide useful information on your website, rather than just selling products or services. This will attract more visitors to your site.

The ability to accept credit cards online is important, and to do this you will need to obtain and set up a merchant account with a bank, but the process is straightforward, and a web designer can advise you on this. The one we use, and recommend is www.worldpay.com.

Of course, marketing on the Internet is a subject by itself and there are many good books that specialise in this topic. Time spent researching and learning the ropes as it were, will pay dividends in the long run.

11

Bonus Items

◆

Offering bonuses to nail the sale

When someone has already made up their mind to make a purchase, the sale is virtually a done deal. In most cases however, you will be promoting something that up until that point, the customer did not realise that they needed.

Convincing someone to buy a product or service is no easy task, especially when they are confronted with advertising from every direction in their daily lives. Most people know when they are being sold to, and they tend to be suspicious—they naturally question whether they really need what they are being offered.

All of this means that when you are selling to a customer "from cold" as it were, your offer needs to be very persuasive. This is where bonuses are helpful.

TV home shopping channels and infomercials are probably the number one users of bonuses. The sales message for most products sold via this method starts by convincing you to invest in a particular product, and the initial approach is surprisingly effective. Some people however, still have a nagging doubt about whether or not to place the order. They see the benefits, and have been convinced of the value of the product, but they need an extra "nudge" in order to commit to the sale. It's at this point that the secret weapon of "bonuses" is unleashed on them.

"Buy this vacuum cleaner today and you will receive *six special attachments for free*" is typical of this kind of offer. "Buy the large kitchen super-mop and *we'll throw in this valuable alarm clock free*" is another example of how a bonus is added.

Psychologically, bonus items work well because they are viewed as just that, extras that are being included for free. The reality of course is that they were simply calculated as part of the overall price in the first place. Even so, it should remind you yet again, how powerful the word "free" is. Hearing that they will receive extra items for "free" will be enough to persuade most hesitant customers to place the order.

Applying the principles to your business:

Could some elements of your complete product package, such as some of the accessories, be separated and marketed as bonuses? Alternatively, could you source some low cost items to use specifically as bonuses—items that compliment what you are already selling, and that could be swallowed within your overall costs? Note that such items should have a high perceived value, otherwise the technique may backfire if the customer thinks that the bonus is worthless. Also, it is generally better to offer two or more lower priced items as bonuses rather than just a single item. Sad to say, for marketing purposes, quantity is usually better than quality in most instances, but feel free to try different combinations to see what works best for you. Also try the offer with and without the bonus(es) to measure and compare the results.

The main secret to using bonuses effectively is to make the customer believe that it's an offer they can't refuse. Also, make sure you withhold the information about the bonuses until near the end of your offer. Make it sound as though it's an afterthought or a late decision to include the bonuses. Try and convey that the customer will be getting your best ever deal.

In general terms, bonuses work best when selling lower priced (less than $250 retail price) goods and services to the mass market. If you are selling specialist, high-end products and services to niche markets, then you probably don't need to use bonuses, because if the customer wants your product enough (and there are few competitors) they will want to (and have to) buy from you anyway. There are no hard and fast rules with marketing however, only guidelines, so feel free to experiment.

12

Celebrity Endorsements

◆

Using well known personalities to endorse your products

Large companies frequently use celebrities to endorse their products and services, and there is no reason why you should not do so too. Why do it? It works! Yes, most people take notice of endorsements from someone they are familiar with.

It's somewhat amusing to consider that even though the vast majority of celebrities involved in recommending a particular product or service are being paid large amounts of money, most consumers forget this, and they are genuinely influenced by the personal recommendation of a high profile personality. The attitude tends to be, "if it's good enough for them, then its good enough for me." Such a recommendation also adds credibility to both the company and the offer, because prospective customers realise that a celebrity would not knowingly recommend something dubious, unproven, or a scam.

There is also a vanity aspect to this. Many people hold prominent public figures in high esteem, and they aspire to achieve something similar with their own lives. Advertising appeals to this selfish desire by getting consumers to think, "if I use this product, I will be as famous/handsome/pretty/desirable/popular/clever" as that person.

There are many well known examples of celebrity endorsement deals: Pop music singers with Pepsi, Sarah Ferguson (Duchess of York) with Weight Watchers, and Michael Jordan with just about every product you can think of!

Applying the principles to your business:

At this point, you might be thinking that the costs involved in using a celebrity would rule it out for the small business. Actually, it may well be more affordable than you might imagine, and there are a number of options that are open to you:

1. Paid or unpaid endorsements, where the celebrity simply states whatever they are asked. This is usually for a specific advertisement, whether in print, radio, or TV. Sorry to shatter your illusions, but most endorsements are pre-scripted and the celebrity simply reads the script.

2. Indirect endorsements, where the celebrity uses your product or service, such as by wearing a line of clothing or footwear. Then when they are photographed or make a public appearance, they are indirectly recommending the product.

3. Paid or unpaid testimonials, where the celebrity genuinely likes the product or service, and is willing to supply a quotation and photo that you can use in your future marketing.

Let's say that the idea of using a celebrity to endorse your product appeals. How do you go about it? The first step is to choose a *suitable* celebrity, because not just anyone will do. For example, how effective do you think it would be for a young and trendy sitcom star, to promote a line of hearing aid products? Conversely, would it be logical for an aging classical opera singer to promote a line of teenage clothing? The two do not go well together. Of course, there are always exceptions, and the apparent mismatch of "celebrity to product" could be used to gain attention for your product. The danger is that the attention could be negative, so be careful.

So what would be a good match? If the product or service involves modern technology, it would be logical to use a television presenter from that field. It would actually add tremendous credibility to your offer, because the perception by the consumer would be that the presenter is *reviewing* the product rather than being paid to recommend it. Likewise if you are selling sports equipment, it would be logical to use a prominent figure from a sporting profession that fits with what you are selling.

It is important not to jump head first into any deal with a celebrity before carefully evaluating what they can offer. You must ask, will this person fit in with the image and philosophy of my company? Are they generally thought of in a positive or negative way? Do the general public like the person, or do they find them irritating? Will they be convincing, or might their recommendation look contrived?

Once you have found a suitable celebrity, you need to contact their agent to first determine whether they are interested or not. There are numerous entertainment guidebooks where you can find the relevant contact information. If in doubt, search the Internet, using the term "celebrity broker". Give as much information as possible about the job, to the agent, and stress that you are a small company. Most agents are willing to negotiate, and you have nothing to lose by stating your budget, whatever that is. As a guide, minor celebrities usually seek a minimum of around £3500 ($5000) plus expenses. Sometimes there are royalty fees in addition, and these are payable each time the endorsement is used.

It is also worth asking around amongst friends, colleagues, in fact anyone you regularly come into contact with, to see if they know any famous people. You will probably be surprised at how many names you can come up with, just by asking everyone you know. Narrow down your list, and depending on how well your contact knows the celebrity, they may be able to help you get a testimonial, or even an endorsement. If you are willing to be flexible, that will help, and remember you have nothing to lose by asking. The problem is that most people don't ask. Think of it this way, if you don't ask, the answer will definitely be no. If you ask, the answer might be yes!

For some celebrities, the offer of free products for a period of time, share options in your company, or whatever else you can negotiate, may be enough on it's own to swing a testimonial. It is also not unheard of for a celebrity to be so genuinely happy with a product or service, that they will recommend it eagerly and enthusiastically without asking for remuneration. If the worst comes to the worst, and all your attempts to win over your first choice of celebrity fails, then try someone else!

If your product is inexpensive, you may want to try mailing out samples to well known celebrities with a simple feedback form that they can easily return to you. Again, if you don't ask, you don't get, and if you keep sending the samples, sooner or later you are sure to obtain some great testimonials from well known personalities. Always remember to ask permission before repeating their comments however; you don't want to face a law suit!

13

Expert Testimonials

✦

How testimony from experts adds credibility to your products

Expert testimonials are similar to celebrity endorsements, but they tend to focus more on the characteristics and specification of the product, or service, that you are selling. Remember, it is human nature to believe what experts tell us. We know that there are experts in every field, and when they say something with authority, we generally have no reason to question them. That's what makes expert testimony so valuable in marketing. It provides immediate credibility, and can be highly persuasive.

As with celebrity endorsements, the individual or recognised body that supplies the expert testimonial should be a good match with what you are selling. For example, if you are promoting a brand of toothpaste, then a senior representative from the dental association or a dentist would be the logical person to recommend the product. If you are promoting a new form of pet food, then it would be ideal if you could get a vet to provide a testimonial.

Expert testimony does not always have to come from someone who is well schooled, or who has many qualifications. It really depends on the field. For example, in the world of hi-fi, let's suppose that a company needs to promote a new CD player. An expert in this context *could* be the editor of a well known trade magazine, an audio technician from the movie industry, a newspaper reviewer, or a record producer. These are just examples, there are many more possibilities. Although not famous (as in a celebrity testimonial), and although they might not be well schooled, the target audience will still view such people as experts, and will respect their experience and authority.

Applying the principles to your business:

Many small businesses would benefit from using the testimony of experts. If your product or service is truly unique or innovative, then you should not have much problem in obtaining some testimonials. Try approaching trade bodies that govern your industry, and explain what you need, they will probably be able to direct you to the most appropriate experts.

If your offer is something that does not necessarily require an expert testimonial, you can still use such individuals to good effect, by asking them to provide a general testimonial. Their name and title alone can carry a lot of weight, even if they are not commenting in their professional capacity. Yes, you can use the fact that many people are easily impressed by someone's status, to your advantage. If using such people, remember to put their full title and the relevant letters after their name wherever possible, for example:

> *"I highly recommend Luigi's Italian restaurant. It is a first class dining experience, and my favourite restaurant in town."*
>
> —Dr Jonathan Frederickson, MD, AMP, DND

There are a few things that you should note about testimonials, whether they are from celebrities, experts or even satisfied customers.

1. Be specific. Generalities are not as powerful as specific statements. For example, "Using Kevin Edward's real estate course, I was in business and making money within two weeks," is far more effective as a testimonial than, "I highly recommend this product."

2. Clearly indicate the exact source of the testimonial. Stating *"Bob Richards"* on its own is not enough. Far better would be:

   "Bob Richards, American Paints Inc, Tampa, Fl."

   Remember, customers are naturally skeptical, and the more information you can provide them about the source of the testimonial, the more believable it will be.

3. If possible, include a photograph of the person who provided the testimonial. This further adds credibility. This will not always be possible, but you really should make every effort to obtain a photograph to go

with each testimonial. Ideally, the photograph should show the person using your product.

14

Using Market Research & Statistics

❖

The influencing power of facts and figures

Many people are easily swayed by facts and figures, as long as they are used in the right circumstances. Realising this, some companies feature statistics or market research in their promotions, in order to reinforce their marketing message and sway opinion to meet a specific objective. We all know that politicians do this regularly. They are known to extract the information that suits their purpose, and feature it in such a way as to influence the population.

Let's take look at some more examples of this technique:

"Tests revealed that our X brand lasts 10 times as long as the Y brand."

"Proven in scientific studies to reduce a fever within 10 minutes."

"Eight out of ten cats preferred our special munchy mix."

"Used by more professional mechanics than any other wrench."

"The fastest growing computer manufacturer in the world."

As you can see, such statements are powerful and persuasive. Of course, if you make a specific claim, you need to be able to back it up with the relevant evidence if challenged.

Some companies have built their entire reputation on statistics. For example, where two major companies with a similar product are competing against each other, if one were to boldly emphasise that they have triple the number of customers compared to the other, that would be a major factor in influencing customers. Human nature means that most consumers will prefer to go with a company that is leading the way, rather than the one that is trailing.

Applying the principles to your business:

In your business, are there any aspects of your products or services that are completely unique, use a special technology, or that excel when compared with the competition? Do you have any useful statistics that could be adapted or simplified to be included with your marketing? Has any market research been carried out that revealed an edge over your competition? Have you won any awards that relate to your business? Such information can be used in a persuasive way to enhance the overall appeal of whatever you are selling.

Consider some examples that could relate to small businesses:

"Voted best restaurant in Newport for four consecutive years."

"As featured on *Channel 5 News* last month."

"Rated in *Gardeners Monthly* as the most useful product of the year."

"3 out of 5 residents use Deans Dry Cleaners."

One of the main tricks to using statistics is to get in there before anyone else does. If you can establish in the marketplace that you lead in some way, that will elevate your company and do a lot of damage to competitors. Even though a competitor may be superior in other ways, your business will still be associated with success.

Look again at the examples above. Although the restaurant that was voted the best in Newport for four years makes a valid claim, it is quite possible that other restaurants also received similar awards from reviews in other publications. However, because the restaurant above made the claim first, it would be foolish for other restaurants to try and make the same claim afterwards. It is very important to stake your claim first!

Make sure that the statistics or market research that you use are relevant to your business. Some companies quote the number of website visitors they have had within a certain period, which is meaningless unless compared with a similar site. Even then, it tends to be perceived as bragging, rather than a persuasive piece of information.

Don't try and blind consumers with science. Whilst you can pull the wool over some peoples eyes, if you try and twist the facts by using complicated language, not only will many people be turned off, you can be sure that sooner or later you will be challenged by someone who has more knowledge of the subject than you do.

The Importance of Including Benefit Statements

Another common mistake in using statistics is to neglect to include a benefit statement. On their own, facts can tend to elicit a "so what" response, which is more harmful than helpful. This is an area where you can soar above the competition, because the inclusion of a benefit statement will dramatically increase the results of your marketing.

Again, consider some of the examples cited previously. With the addition of a benefit statement, look at how much more persuasive they are:

"Voted best restaurant in Newport for four consecutive years, which means you are guaranteed to have an enjoyable meal."

"Rated in *Gardeners Monthly* as the most useful product of the year. The decision is made for you!"

"3 out of 5 residents use Deans Dry Cleaners—for good reason. We treat your clothes as if they were our own."

"Tests revealed that our X brand lasts 10 times as long as the Y brand. Yes, you'll get much more for your money with X brand."

"Proven in scientific studies to reduce a fever within 10 minutes, that's twice as fast as the nearest competitor."

"Eight out of ten cats preferred our special munchy mix. Don't waste your money on inferior cat food."

"Used by more professional mechanics than any other wrench. When your tools need to be consistently reliable, there is no other choice."

Can you see the improvement? If you are in doubt about how to add the benefit statement to the statistic or market research, it is often helpful to use the phrase, "which means to you…" as a link. If the resulting phrase does not sound natural, it may be that the first phrase is not suitable. In the example of, "we are the fastest growing computer manufacturer in the world," it is very difficult to come up with a benefit statement that corresponds to the initial phrase. To say that you are the fastest growing company might be impressive to yourself and your peers, but it tends to elicit a "so what" response from consumers. Beware of this pitfall.

15

Sponsorship

◆

An effective "back door" method of marketing

When you think of the word sponsorship, what picture do you have in your mind? You will probably think one of two ways. You will either imagine sponsoring a friend or family member to complete some task for charity (such as in the case of a sponsored walk), or you will conjure up images of sports stars and other personalities that command millions in sponsorship money, by simply agreeing to wear a particular brand of clothing and pose for some photographs. In the context of marketing your business, we are obviously dwelling on the latter type of sponsorship (without the high costs).

One of the great things about sponsorship is that it's often more subtle than other forms of promotion or advertising. Rarely is sponsorship "in your face" as a direct sales message. Even the seemingly blatant: "this message is brought to you by…" style of announcement on TV or radio still has a somewhat "soft" edge to it. The fact that the message has been "brought to you" by a particular company seems to be a positive thing; we feel that we should be somewhat grateful to the company for arranging that.

Some of the largest corporations in the world use sponsorship as a way to subtly influence what we buy. Sports teams often wear the logos of well known companies on their clothing, soft drinks manufacturers such as Pepsi and Coca Cola often sponsor events such as music concerts, and product placement has become an integral part of movies and TV shows. All these methods of marketing products are a "soft sell" because unless we stop to think about it, we don't naturally consider them to be advertising.

The thinking behind who or what to sponsor is often very calculated, and you can learn from this. Take McDonald's, for example. They sponsor organisations on a local and national level that benefit young children. This is not accidental.

McDonald's knows that their future customers are made up largely of the young children of today, so they are a logical target audience. That's not to take away from the support that McDonald's provides, which is valuable and appreciated, but at the same time, they ensure that the money they spend has some benefit to the company further down the line. That's business.

Sponsorship does not always have to be in the form of goods and services of course. Monetary sponsorship is always appreciated by needy organisations, as they can use the money for a function of their choice, whereas the donation of a product or service, whilst appreciated, may not always be suitable.

Applying the principles to your business:

Sponsorship is often overlooked as a method of marketing, but it can be very valuable to the small business. It involves offering your products, services or even money to another business, organisation or charity that seeks support. In return, your company receives recognition and promotional opportunities.

Let's say you own a local printing business in a small town. There are numerous opportunities for sponsorship that could benefit you. It might be as simple as agreeing to print the programmes for the next production of a local drama group. In return for doing that, your company could have a large advert in the programme, a prominent credit on the posters, on the tickets, and so on. It's a win-win situation.

There are two main reasons this kind of marketing could be effective for you. Firstly, your company will be perceived in a positive way by people who live locally. You will be seen to be entering into the spirit of the community, because of your willingness to "help" a local organisation. Secondly, the resulting publicity can actually be worth more to you, than if you had purchased it through traditional methods. Conventional advertising is expensive, and many consumers have learnt to switch off from it, so sponsorship is one way you can reach them "through the back door" as it were.

Let's take another example. Suppose you have a small business that offers financial advice and insurance services. That kind of business may not seem suitable as a sponsorship provider, but in truth, most businesses can make sponsorship work. For example, you could offer to sponsor a local sports team by providing them with discounted insurance, financial advice, and even monetary aid. Don't assume that the club will demand more than you are planning to provide. Many organisations will take whatever they can, which often costs very little for businesses to provide.

Getting Full Value from Sponsorship

Whatever sponsorship you get involved in, don't shy away from getting the full value from it, however simple it might seem. For example, let's imagine you are sponsoring to keep a section of road clean in your area. Don't be content with the standard sign along the lines of: "this section of road cleaned by…" If you have a company newsletter, write about it in there. If there is a humorous or interesting story behind how you came to decide on the sponsorship, then write it up and submit it to the local newspaper. Tell your customers about it, using every means possible. In every case, aim to maximise the usefulness of the sponsorship.

When considering a sponsorship offer, or when contemplating who to approach with an offer of sponsorship, make sure there is a natural, logical tie-in with the product or service you are offering. In simple terms, ensure that the sponsorship will benefit your company! Sponsorship of the wrong organisation is pointless. For example, if you own a shop that sells video games to teenagers, there is little point in agreeing to provide sponsorship money to the local gardeners' society. However worthy the cause, the two just don't fit. If you are feeling charitable, then by all means contribute to any worthy cause you like, just be aware of the implications of sponsoring an organisation that is a poor match to your products or services.

In order to be certain of a good fit between yourself as the sponsor and the client, ask yourself, who are my target customers? Which products do they use regularly? Which products could I encourage them to use?

You should also make sure that both parties are clear about what they are giving, and what they will be getting. Make sure this is in writing. If the arrangement turns sour because of a misunderstanding, you might unwittingly find yourself with a bad reputation, especially in a local community where everyone talks to each other.

16

Remain Fresh and Innovative

◆

*How to stop your products
(and business) becoming stagnant*

If you have managed to launch a successful product or service, it is very tempting to stick with it rigidly, and never divert from it. The danger however, is that eventually your product or service may be perceived as dull or old-fashioned. It is important to keep your company fresh and innovative, even "reinventing" what you offer from time to time. Let's look at some ways that a few large companies have done this.

McDonald's and other fast food chains are known to use a formulaic approach in their business. They have systems in place for just about every aspect of running the business, but crucially, when it comes to the menu items, they are willing to introduce new foods and flavours regularly. Why? Very simply, to keep customers coming back.

Over the years, McDonald's has steadily introduced a variety of new items to their menu. Not a year goes by without changes of some sort. Then too, there are special temporary menus that appear from time to time, often themed by a link up with a new movie, or featuring tastes from other countries. Other innovations in recent years have included the ever changing happy meals for kids, the choices menu, and the dollar menu in the USA. In addition, on a global scale McDonald's has reacted to the varying needs of different cultures and countries by introducing special menu items that are country specific. This means that each country has its own special items, designed to appeal to the culture of that region.

A Warning Lesson

Reinventing or repositioning a brand name does not always work in a positive way however, as the experience of Coca-Cola, the well known drinks brand showed. Most drinks manufacturers have at some point introduced a change in the ingredients, in order to improve the taste. That is a common strategy, and for the most part it works well. The problem with the Coca-Cola example was that the drink is such an integral part of America's culture that the company did not take into account the strong public feeling towards it. So what happened?

In 1985 Coca-Cola tried to change their established, best selling formula, by introducing a radical, new type of Cola in its place. In my view, and the view of many others, what they should have done was enhance the *existing* brand, by adding another product that would *complement* their best seller. Instead, they chose to change the much loved Coca-Cola.

So what happened? Well, since its outset, Coca-Cola had been the "real thing," but with the introduction of this "new Coke" suddenly it was *not* the real thing. The company had decided to reposition the product from being a reliable, solid, "you always know what you are going to get" type of brand, to a "new" product, one that in the consumers eyes was untested, unproven and inferior.

The strong public feeling to "new Coke" was nothing short of incredible. Customers felt betrayed, and vocalised this feeling by stating that their years of loyalty to the "real thing" had been for nothing. The overwhelming reaction by consumers was, "what right do they have to mess with our drink?"

The end result of this marketing blunder was to reintroduce the original coke under a new name, "Classic Coke" (which was a clever move), but within the few short months that "new Coke" had been in the marketplace, a lot of damage had already been done.

In recent years both Pepsi and Coca-Cola have experimented with reasonable success in introducing products to compliment rather than replace their main brands. They are continually trying to keep things fresh and innovative.

As an example, with so much emphasis on eating healthily and taking care of oneself, when diet versions of Cola drinks were launched, sales rocketed. Other variations that have been introduced with varying success include Vanilla Coke, Cherry Coke, Caffeine free Coke, Pepsi Twist, Pepsi One and Wild Cherry Pepsi. The important thing to remember is that all of these subsidiary brands have gained additional sales for the company, they have kept the overall brand in front of the customer, and they have demonstrated that the companies involved want to provide products that reflect the ever changing needs of their customers.

Let's take another example. If theme parks like Disney did not regularly replace or add new rides and attractions, the majority of people would probably only visit once or twice in their lifetime. The draw of new attractions is substantial, and many people will base their decision to return to a theme park, on the addition of even a single major ride that has been added since their last visit. Of course, the marketing teams know this, and they spend vast amounts of money on letting us all know that the latest attraction is the best ever, and that we will be missing out if we don't experience it for ourselves.

As a final example, Starbucks, the coffee house, also endeavours to be seen as innovating and keeping things fresh. Whilst the core menu remains the same, new items are added regularly, and special products are offered on a temporary basis, according to the season. In the winter, beverages such as warm apple cider appear on the menu, and in the summer, variations of frappuccinos (blended drinks), are also introduced. This means that there is always something new on offer.

Applying the principles to your business:

It's a good idea to ask your staff, colleagues and friends how they perceive your company. Do they consider it to be innovative and progressive, or could it be fairly accused of being in a rut, with little innovation to speak of?

Would it be feasible to produce some variations of your existing services or products? Have customers ever asked for such variations? You might want to conduct a survey to gauge the demand.

Let's suppose you own a restaurant. When was the last time you added new items to your menu? If you have daily specials, how do you feature them? Are customers even aware of them?

One trend that seems to be increasingly popular in many western countries is the low-carb diet, such as Atkins. Although some consider it to be a fad, this kind of diet appears to be gaining in popularity amongst large sections of the population. Have you considered catering to the needs of the increasing numbers of people who are on this kind of diet? This is an example of a trend that should be reacted to proactively and quickly, rather than waiting for others to lead. If you don't, you WILL lose customers. Consider the positive benefits of the low carb diet example—if you were the only restaurant in your town to prominently feature special menu items for this type of popular diet, you would win a lot of business.

Such innovation is not just desirable, it is essential. If you don't give attention to making consistent improvements with your products and services, you could easily be overtaken and get left behind. That's the nature of business. There will always be someone else out there that has similar ambitions to you, but with a fresh approach, a different way of thinking. That's why you need to aim to be one step ahead.

Extending the Principle to All Aspects of Your Business

Of course, the quest to remain fresh and innovative should apply to all aspects of your business, not only in the products and services you offer. For example, do you regularly review the methods you use for ordering, packing, delivery, customer service, and so on? Literally every aspect of your business should be reviewed from time to time to see where improvements can be made.

It might be that you find a new supplier to handle your deliveries. If they are more reliable and cheaper, not only could you pass some additional savings on to customers, but you could win more business by being more efficient. From personal experience, there are some companies that I would like to use, but don't, solely because they only offer a slow shipping option. They are losing out on a lot of business.

Perhaps your current method of providing quotations is slow. By making some adjustments to offer quotes via email, the process would be more efficient *and* save money.

Your current method of packaging might also benefit from a review. If you are sending delicate items that have a high rate of breakage, there may be a more suitable product that will protect the goods more efficiently. Remember, happy customers usually remain loyal customers.

In all these fields, new innovations that could benefit your company are announced every day. Keep alert to these and consider them seriously from time to time. The old method of doing something may not necessarily be the best.

In general terms, the USA is a good example of a country that has remained fresh and innovative in business, never afraid to try new things. Granted, there have been some ideas that have failed spectacularly, but for the most part consumers benefit. Over the years, consumers have embraced innovations that are now taken for granted, such as the drive-thru, ATM machines in small stores, credit card processing at the gas pump, microwave ovens, and so on.

The lesson then, is to question all aspects of your business to see if there might be a better way. Sometimes you will discover cost savings, sometimes it will be time savings, and sometimes you will discover ways of enhancing the customer experience. All of these are good reasons to implement a change.

17

Care about Colour

✦

How colour affects consumer buying decisions

Corporations and large businesses often spend a small fortune on choosing appropriate colours to use in their logo, packaging, or marketing materials. This might seem like a waste of money, and in many cases the amount of money involved is obscene, but there is more to this than you might think.

Apparently the human eye can distinguish over three million subtle variations of colour, which is a staggering statistic, and it's been proven that different colours do have noticeable effects on us, whether we realise it or not. For example, yellow is the best colour for grabbing attention, it stands out from the crowd more than any other colour. Blue and green are proven to be calming colours, whereas red is lively and excites. Interestingly, suicides dropped a staggering 34% after London's Blackfriars Bridge was painted green.

Colours have the ability to make us happy, sad, angry, content, or virtually any other emotion. They can make us hungry, or influence us to lose our appetite. Colours can raise or lower blood pressure. You get the idea.

Interestingly, colours can have different meanings according to variations in countries or regions. In China, white is the colour of mourning, so it would not be suitable for a brides wedding dress. In France, yellow signifies jealousy. In many far eastern lands, green is considered a sacred colour. In Brazil, purple is the colour of death, whereas in Japan it symbolises luxury.

For a moment, think about how well established brands use colour. How about the vibrant red on a can of Coke? The distinctive pink colour of the Financial Times newspaper? The bright yellow of the Yellow Pages directory? Or the expensive looking gold top of Duracell batteries? These colour choices are not accidental.

It is apparent then that in business, your choice of colour is important. Here is a brief summary of some of the main characteristics of popular colours:

Red: Power, sex, impulse buying, danger, stop, aggressive, hot, competitive, passion, speed

Yellow: Fun, youthful, warning, construction, telephone directories, frivolous, optimistic

Pink: Innocent, fragile, feminine, business oriented, suppresses appetite, secure

Green: Money, nature, jealousy, luck, politics, environmental, cool, abundant, safety

Brown: Reliable, dependable, neutral, genuine, sad, meditative

Purple: Leadership, Royal, spiritual, dignified

Blue: Cool, calm, authoritative, status, trustworthy, enduring, reliable, loyal, dignified

Orange: youthful, modern, energetic, fun, passionate, stimulates appetite

White: clean, youthful, mild, virginal, pure, sterile, empty, light

Black: Sophistication, elegance, seductive, mysterious, dependable, timeless

Silver: Scientific, cold, prestigious, technical

Gold: Expensive, prestigious, quality, luxury, lavish

Applying the principles to your business:

Since choice of colour has the ability to both increase and decrease sales, it deserves your attention. Could it be that your current choice and use of colours within your business has been influenced more by personal preference than any psychological reasons or research?

On examination, many small businesses have discovered that their use of colour sends out mixed messages. For instance, one designer may have been used to develop some marketing materials, another for packaging, and still another for stationery and business cards. The result of this is usually a clash of conflicting messages. Imagine if each branch of a major chain of stores were given free reign to design their own logos and colour schemes? What would the result be? Customers would likely have trouble identifying the brand, and they would quickly lose confidence in it. Don't do the same with your business. Choose colours carefully, and be consistent.

Your first step is to identify which colour or colours fit well with the ideologies of your products and services. What type of image do you want to convey? If you are in an industry that struggles to be taken seriously, perhaps brown, purple or blue would help to overcome that stigma. If your business seems to be considered too serious, you might want to inject some fun, by using a shade of orange.

It's also worth noting that colours, like fashion, go through trends, albeit at a slower rate of change. At any particular time, some colours will be more popular than others. It's well worth taking some time to see how other companies are using colour. If you see a particular shade you on a document or brochure that you feel is suitable, you could scan the item, and use software such as Photoshop to ascertain the Pantone number of the colour. Again, let us emphasise that you should not be influenced purely by personal taste. Make sure that the colours you choose are right psychologically for your business.

Interestingly, the choice of colours extends further than you might think. As well as the many broad choices, there are virtually infinite shades, hues, and levels of brightness that provide an even wider choice. A business that specialises in producing video games for young people will likely feature strong, bright colours, whereas a business that is involved in healthcare will probably opt for the use of soft, pastel shades. Bear in mind too, with modern advances in printing, it is possible to print true gold and silver colours for a small premium in cost.

On a practical note, keep in mind that the number of colours you use will have a significant impact on the costs of preparing and printing marketing materials. Full colour documents will always be much more expensive than using a single colour. When you are ready to print, always get as many quotes as you can, because you will find that printing is one industry where costs can vary considerably. It's also worth familiarising yourself with some of the more commonly used expressions in the trade, such as bleed, border, blueline proof, lithography, offset, and colour separation. If you can speak the same "language" as the printer, you are more likely to get exactly what you want, at the right price. In short, they will take you seriously, because they know that you know what you are talking about.

Whatever colour choices you settle on, it is preferable to have one designer take care of all materials that are produced, so as to keep a consistent approach. Brand recognition is vital, and if your marketing materials follow a consistent approach, you will win more customers over time.

18

Educate Your Buyers

◆

Getting customers to think like you think

We have dwelt a lot on satisfying the demands of customers, but sometimes it is possible to *educate* customers in such a way that they desire your products or services. This is sometimes referred to as mindset marketing, because the idea is to change the customer's mindset, or way of thinking, so that they are receptive to your products or services.

One of the best examples of a company that has done this effectively is Nike, the sports shoe manufacturer. At one time, Nike was seen as a brand for the young, athletic, and trendy person. They have done such a good job of mindset marketing however, that it is now not uncommon to see old ladies alongside skateboarding youths, *both* wearing Nike shoes. The mindset Nike created was that their products are not about youth; rather they are a universal commodity that everyone should possess.

Let's take another example. After the BSE (mad cow disease) crisis in the UK, meat distributors in that country had an uphill battle in changing the mindset of both the population as well as foreign importers of British beef. Eventually this happened, and as a result, few people subsequently dwelt on the dangers of eating beef.

In the U.S., a company that has done a good job of educating customers is Radio Shack. They realised that when it comes to electronics, many people have an interest in gadgets and technical things, but they lack knowledge. Radio Shack has hammered home the marketing message that, "you've got questions, we've got answers." In other words, they have gone out of their way to help educate their customers. As a result of more knowledge, the customer is generally more inclined to buy the product, and they are also more inclined to return to a store where they are encouraged to ask questions and seek information.

The facility to search for, and download a product manual from the convenience of the Radio Shack website is another tool that has won them more customers. The website also features "how to" guides and support documents that are invaluable. Radio Shack is now known as the helpful, friendly store to buy electronics from.

Applying the principles to your business:

There are two main elements of educating customers by marketing. This involves (a) notifying the customer that the product or service exists, and (b) helping them to see that it will be of value to them.

Taking the first aspect of notifying the customer that the product or service exists, this sounds obvious, but I have lost count of the number of times that people have said to me, "If only there were a product that could….." The frustrating thing is that in most cases, there *will* be a product that solves the stated problem, but the consumer does not know that it exists, because the relevant company has not done a good job of educating them about it.

Educational marketing of this nature can take on many different forms. You could write an article for a magazine or newspaper, volunteer your expertise for a radio or TV interview, write a book, build a website, and so on.

Suppose that you had developed a solution to a very specific problem that affects a particular type of person or industry. As we said, it is quite possible that the target audience might not realise that the problem exists. In that case, you need to educate them about the problem *first,* before you can present the solution. This is actually another form of mindset marketing.

Adobe, who are one of the world's largest software companies, produced an excellent piece of software called Acrobat. Primarily, it is used for distributing electronic documents between computer users. However, Adobe realised that very few people realised what else Acrobat could be used for, so they embarked on an ambitious program to educate their key resellers and distributors. The face to face training worked, and as a result, computer users in general are becoming more aware of the full potential of this software.

Could it be that your customers or distributors would benefit from a training session, a video or DVD tutorial, or some other form of educational material? In some retail stores customers can see live presentations or taped materials that educate customers as to the benefits of the product.

Another value of educating customers relates to when the customer knows they need a product or service, but they don't necessarily understand it. Recall the Radio Shack example. Armed with the right knowledge, buyers tend to be more comfortable about spending their hard earned money.

Think about ways that you can supply useful, practical knowledge to customers in your industry. Be seen to be helpful rather than just clamouring after the sale. Remember, you should be seeking long term loyalty, not just a one off sale.

You should be aware that not all efforts to educate consumers are honourable. It is very common for companies to focus on the benefits of their product whilst neglecting to mention some serious down sides. A soft drink may be marketed as containing a major source of Vitamins, but the company may fail to mention that it is also loaded with sugar and harmful additives. In the advertising world this kind of technique is known as card stacking. In other words, the company stacks the cards in favour of the product they are promoting, stressing all of the good points about it, whilst conveniently overlooking the negatives.

On the positive side again, educating consumers also gives you the ability to up-sell them to a higher priced product or service. Let's say that you sell mobile phones. A customer might approach you with the intent of purchasing a simple phone. By gauging their reaction to carefully worded questions, you might determine that a higher priced phone would actually be more suitable for them. However, if the customer is not aware of the higher specified product, or they don't understand it, you would likely lose the sale. Provide the customer with solid evidence why the product would be preferable for them, and it's quite likely that they can be persuaded to go for the more expensive alternative.

At the time of writing, digital video recorders (DVR's) are becoming popular, and a few years down the line we will probably look back and wonder how we ever watched TV without them. These devices enable the viewer to manage multi-channel TV in a far easier and more productive way. Users can pause, rewind and fast forward live television, record an entire series with the press of a button, record several programmes on different channels at the same time, and so on. Some of the advanced units, such as the popular "*TIVO,*" even have the facility to automatically record all programmes that feature a favourite actor or actress.

Virtually everyone who has a DVR raves about how good it is, yet it is a very difficult concept to explain—it really needs to be demonstrated. Knowing that the public were slow to catch on to the usefulness of these units, one enterprising cable company offered their own brand of DVR to all customers as a matter of course, whenever their technicians made a house call. The technicians simply encouraged the home owner to try the service, saying that if they liked it, they could keep the box for a small monthly fee, and if they did not want it they could return it without charge. Needless to say, in most cases, as soon as the box was installed and the viewer realised how useful it was, they ended up keeping it.

Could you do something similar in your industry? Whilst it may not be practical to provide every customer with a high tech product to try, you might consider offering such an item to certain companies in your distribution channel, so that they can make a direct recommendation to customers or end users.

Service industries can also educate their distribution channel. For example, travel agents are often offered educational trips, sometimes known as a "FAM" (short for familiarisation). Usually these trips are co-sponsored by an airline, a tour operator and a hotel chain, with the aim of letting travel agents experience these services first hand. The companies involved know that if the agents have a good time, they will happily recommend the companies to their customers. An agent who has actually visited Disneyland in Florida for example, is far more likely to be enthusiastic about it than an agent who has not been there. Education works!

19

Keeping up with the Jones'

✦

Marketing that satisfies the
"I want what you have" desire

Few of us want to be considered unusual. We like to be accepted, and when it comes to our buying decisions, we naturally tend to buy what we know others have bought before us. Yes, established brands will always be more popular than brands we have never heard of.

There is also a certain type of person that must have the latest of everything. They like to lead the way, and they like it when others are envious of them. Not everyone is like this of course, but the two groups combined definitely warrant your attention.

Taking the second group first, that is those who must have the latest of everything, it appears as though some industries are more suited to cater for these types of people more than others. For example, technology is a prime example. Computer manufacturers could release major updates of processors and other hardware annually, or even semi-annually, and leave it at that. They know however that many individuals are determined to always have the best, and if they release incremental improvements, it goes without saying that a reasonable number of people will rush to buy the "new" top of the range each time. The rationale on the part of the companies selling these items is: if the customers are there, and they are willing to buy, then why not sell to them?

In the motor industry, vehicle manufacturers put a great deal of emphasis on the annual improvements that are made to each model. Although it is much cheaper to buy a nearly new car, most people want the very latest model. It is important to them that they are seen with a brand new car, so as to impress their friends with the latest features and specification. Manufacturers gladly oblige, and each year, new models are added to the line up to satisfy the insatiable demand of car buyers.

Another prominent example of this type of marketing can be seen in the software industry. Most software companies continually offer upgraded versions of the same program, as a never ending cycle. In a relatively short space of time, Microsoft offered Windows 3.1, then Windows '95, followed by Windows '98, Windows ME, Windows 2000, and Windows XP. Were all these variations essential? Probably not, but Microsoft do a good job of marketing to computer users, and appear to strongly imply that if the customers do not upgrade to the latest version, they will be missing out. Each time new, upgraded software goes on sale, that becomes the standard, and there is a certain amount of unseen pressure on consumers to conform to the new standard.

The same way of thinking extends to other sectors of retail too. How many children must have the same toy that everyone else is getting at Christmas time? How many teenagers must be seen wearing a particular brand of clothing in order not to be teased at school? How many adults are influenced to go and see a certain movie in order that they are not the only ones in their office who have not seen it? That kind of influence and pressure is exerted on us all the time.

It's also appropriate to include the "fear of missing out" factor in this section. Disney has used this technique to good effect in some of their video and DVD releases in recent years. For example, they made it clear in their marketing that certain titles would be offered for a short time only, before being removed from sale. This caused instant demand, and a surge of sales within a short space of time, rather than spreading sales over an extended period. Customers were also reminded that these limited edition DVD's could become collectors items in the future. It was a clever approach, and it certainly seemed to work.

Applying the principles to your business:

Is there a way that you can build your product or service up in the minds of consumers, to the point where it will be considered an essential purchase? Can you position it as more trendy, or reinforce its appeal within a certain market? Could you set a deadline on its sale, so that there is a fear of losing out? Could you market limited edition versions of popular products?

Some of the above can be achieved within your advertising and promotional efforts. If your product includes cutting edge technology, or is the best in its class, make sure you state that prominently in your literature and advertisements. I saw a clever advertisement for a home theatre receiver in a specialist magazine. The ad simply stated, *"Our new receiver makes every other receiver in this magazine redundant."* Strictly speaking it wasn't true, because many people would be perfectly happy to purchase a cheaper system, but from a marketing point of view, it made the product stand out as the best of the best. If money was no object, that would be the product to buy.

Although the ethics of doing so may be questioned by some, you may choose to go down a similar route to computer manufacturers, who as mentioned earlier, offer incremental upgrades and improvements in their products, in order to guarantee a steady stream of sales as each new advance is made. In a similar way, you might choose to "save" (more accurately read as withhold) some improvements in your product for a later time, knowing that some customers always want the best, and are prepared to pay for the latest edition.

A great way to make use of the natural "I want what you have" desire is to distribute a "recommend a friend" offer to your existing customers. This involves inviting existing customers to refer someone else to your products and services. You could do this by email or by sending out a simple reply paid card. The major benefit in doing this is that the friend in each case tends to reason, "If my friend has benefited from buying from that company, I guess I will too, and I don't want to miss out." Naturally, you should provide some incentive for both parties if possible. For example, you could offer a discount to the person who was referred, and some other bonus for the person did the referring. Imagine if just 30 percent of your customers each referred a friend in this way—it is a very cheap way of acquiring new customers.

If you produce a variety of products that are constantly changing, you could try offering limited editions of those items. Build each offer up by elaborating on how unique it is, and state a deadline after which it will not be available. That way you can run such offers throughout the year and build sales by way of the customer's fear of missing out.

A danger to be aware of in this type of marketing is implying that your potential customers cannot think for themselves. If consumers believe that you are saying that of them, they will be immediately turned off from buying. It stands to reason then that balance is needed. On the one hand you want people to believe that they should buy what others are buying, but at the same time you want them to believe that they are making the choice themselves.

20

Putting it all Together

◆

It's time for action!

The mere fact that you have taken the trouble to read this book through from start to finish shows that you are serious about improving the profitability of your business. That puts you in the minority. The reality is that most small business owners spend more time on planning a vacation than they do on planning their business strategy. Sad to say, most of those businesses will fail. These days, intense competition combined with a high level of consumer awareness, means that you cannot afford to treat marketing lightly.

At this point, let's recap on what we have learnt, by way of a summary.

In the introduction, it was explained that marketing plays an essential role in every business. After all, you might have the best product on the planet, but if no one knows about it, your business will go nowhere.

In the first chapter we looked at the power of a simple, four letter word: "FREE." By regularly incorporating free offers in to your marketing efforts, whether they are giveaways, samples, free shipping and so on, you can attract and keep many more customers than you currently have.

The next chapter had the theme, "Make them pay." This section examined the benefits of outsourcing costs to your customers, and a number of examples were given of companies that had done this very successfully, without any negative reaction from consumers.

The need to keep in regular contact with your customers was highlighted in Chapter three. Since it costs a reasonable amount to attract customers in the first place, your business can easily become more profitable by focusing your marketing efforts on *existing* customers, rather than continually spending a fortune on attracting new customers.

In most businesses, complaints are seen as a very negative thing, and in one sense that's true. However, when handled correctly, every complaint has the potential to result in a more loyal customer, and that is a very powerful proposition. That's not to say that complaints should be encouraged, but it does highlight the fact that when they do occur, all is not lost.

Chapter five highlighted the vital need to be different with your marketing. There is no way around this—in order to be effective, marketing has to cut through the "noise" that is generated by other advertisers. Creative advertising is still quite rare these days amongst small businesses, and this is an area where you can definitely gain an edge over your competition, winning more customers as a result. Don't be afraid to try out unusual and creative concepts. If it's different, it's more likely to be remembered.

Another fundamental rule of marketing was discussed in the next chapter, namely to give the customer what *they* want, rather than what *you want to give them*. This is one of the most costly mistakes that businesses make. Learn to focus on customers needs, and you will avoid the same mistake.

Chapter seven reminded us of the need to go with the flow, rather than working against it. We saw how dramatic changes in consumer interests occur over time, and how you should react to those changes. If your company does not embrace change and keep moving with the times, you *will* get left behind.

In the section on joint ventures, you were encouraged to look for suitable partnerships. Ideally, this should be from among businesses that could offer products and services that complement what you already do.

Next we examined the possibility of expanding your business into new geographic areas, as well as broadening the type of customer that you sell to. Using the examples of the fast food chains, it was illustrated how easily a single, local, fast food restaurant could grow into a national and even international chain. The sky's the limit when you open up your business to new geographic locations.

Chapter ten focused on the power of the Internet, to enable you to sell products and services directly to the consumer. Never before has it been so easy to reach so many customers globally, for so little cost. If you have not previously considered selling direct, you should definitely look at the opportunity, even if you also wish to retain your existing distribution channels.

Offering bonus items to nail the sale was the subject of Chapter eleven. Bonus items do not have to cost a lot, but their perceived value to the customer must be high. Bonus items offered as free extras really can make a difference in influencing more customers buy.

Celebrity endorsements and expert testimonials can also have a profound effect on influencing customers to buy, and we looked at ways to obtain these without great expense. A recommendation from a well known or respected source will always increase the number of customers that decide to buy. Along similar lines, market research and statistics can similarly add credibility, to reassure consumers that you are a legitimate company, offering products or services that live up to their claims.

Since traditional advertising is rarely effective these days, sponsoring an organisation or individual can sometimes enable you to reach customers that might otherwise not notice your traditional advertising. Therefore, all sponsorship opportunities deserve your careful consideration.

On a more general note, remaining fresh and innovative in all your marketing is vital to your success. We saw how much times have changed over the years, and how important it is to keep up to date with trends that might affect your business.

The importance of colour was stressed in Chapter seventeen. Although this section was merely a glimpse into how different colours can affect our emotions, you should have learnt that the choice of colours in your marketing materials, packaging, and so on can have a dramatic effect on sales.

Although buyers often lead trends in buying, it is possible for the small business owner to lead customers down a particular path by educating them. Examples were given to show how, over a period of time, the mindset of potential customers can be altered so as to encourage them to think a certain way. If you are currently struggling in your marketplace, it may be that you need to re-educate your customers about the benefits of what you offer.

In some industries, it is possible to encourage customers to buy new versions and upgrades of existing products by instilling a fear of losing out. Many individuals like to brag about having the best of this or that, and if such a desire seems to exist in your marketplace, why not give the customer what they want? It means more sales!

Measuring Your Results

You have seen by now that there are few rules in marketing. Many of the most successful campaigns are the ones that dared to be different. To ensure your long-term success, it is vital to measure the results of every marketing effort. Think about it, if you leave it to chance, you will never know for sure what works and what doesn't. If a particular approach is shown to bring in substantially more business, it stands to reason that you will want to continue that method, but you will only know that by measuring your results.

So how can you gauge the results of a marketing campaign? One way is to include a unique offer code in your marketing materials. It can be anything you like, as long as you keep a record of what campaign it relates to. When they respond to an offer, you instruct the customers to quote the code, which you then record on your database. With multiple codes in use at any one time for a variety of marketing campaigns, it is then a relatively simple matter of keeping track of which offers are the most effective.

Will You Take Action?

As promised, you now have nineteen magical marketing methods, to help increase the sales of your small business. Are they magical? The answer to that depends on what you do with them. The businesses that apply the techniques are likely to see astonishing results. Those that don't will continue to bemoan that marketing does not work!

Be realistic about what you want to achieve, but don't be too easy on yourself. Being in business is hard work, there are no shortcuts. When setbacks occur, keep focused, and keep going. Face the fact that things won't always go well for you. Disappointments are as much a part of life as the thrills and excitement, but it's the way you *deal* with the disappointments that will make you a winner.

Bear in mind too, that whatever mistakes you may have made in the past, have no relevance to your future success. One famous motivational speaker often says: "the past does not equal the future." If you have failed at a venture in the past (and most people have), start afresh with a renewed determination to succeed.

Learning from Walt Disney

A classic example of someone who never gave up was Walt Disney. Here was a man who dreamt up what was considered at the time to be a "preposterous idea" of building an entertainment park with rides and attractions in a remote area of Southern California.

Walt went to the banks to seek funding, and explained his idea that he would charge people one entrance fee, with all the attractions included in that price. The banks consistently told him it was a ridiculous idea. They simply could not envisage that people would be willing to pay one entrance price for an amusement park, as it had never been done before.

How many times was Disney turned down? 302 times! Imagine that.

How many banks would *you* have approached before giving up? Perhaps now you can see the determination and persistence that characterised Disney. Look at what the Disney theme park empire is made up of now: huge theme parks in California, Florida, Paris and Tokyo! Was it worth the persistence? You can answer that yourself.

Of course, the information in this publication is only a start, and you should continue studying as many books on sales, marketing, and advertising as you can. The most successful people in the world make a habit of continuing to learn, and you should too. Be open minded to new ideas and ways of doing things, and not only will your business grow rapidly, you will have a lot of fun in the process.

I wish you every success in your business venture.

Additional Resources

Examples of companies using free offers:

www.britmusic.co.uk

www.bmgmusic.com

www.aol.com

Internet Services:

www.register.com—Popular for registering domain names and web hosting

www.google.com—The most popular search engine on the Internet

www.worldpay.com—Company that helps you set up to accept credit card transactions

Paul Daniels:

www.pauldaniels.co.uk—Official website

www.pauldanielsmagicshop.com—Selling magic tricks, books and videos.

Marketing Resources:

www.freeway101.com—Marketing resources from Jay Conrad Levinson

www.marketingsource.com—General resources from Concept Marketing Inc

marketing.about.com—Forums and articles that focus on marketing

Further reading:

Small Business Marketing for Dummies by Barbara Findlay Schenck

Big Business Marketing For Small Business Budgets by Jeanette Maw McMurtry

How to Make Millions with Your Ideas by Dan Kennedy

Getting Everything You Can Out of all You've Got by Jay Abraham

0-595-30942-9

www.ingramcontent.com/pod-product-compliance
Lightning Source LLC
Chambersburg PA
CBHW030907180526
45163CB00004B/1747